LOFOTEN
TRAVEL GUIDE
2024

Unveiling Norway's Untamed Paradise,
discover everyday local life with a global
interest in its natural beauty

Blevins D. Hammond

Copyright © 2024 Blevins D. Hammond

Notice of Disclaimer

This book's content is intended to give readers useful knowledge about the topics covered. The guidebook makes no claims about the authenticity of the information or recommendations it offers; its sole purpose is to give the reader an overview of the fundamental travel rules for a particular area. Before leaving, each traveler should conduct independent research.

TABLE OF CONTENTS

INTRODUCTION

Lofoten Islands: A Magical Archipelago on the World's Periphery

Lofoten Islands, where craggy peaks pierce the sky and the aurora borealis paints the skies in a plethora of heavenly colors. Here, fishing communities cling tenaciously to the beach while the North Atlantic Ocean slams against granite cliffs. This is a country of raw, untamed beauty. Get ready to be mesmerized by a world where nature rules supreme and time appears to slow down.

My Story of Love in Lofoten:

Years ago, the allure of Lofoten drew me in with tales of Viking sagas and scenery carved by glaciers. The sharp Arctic air awoke my senses as soon as I got aboard the ship, and the sight of the very high mountains, known as "," took my breath away. That was it; I was hooked.

I have been to every corner of this enchanted archipelago over the years, from the secluded, bird-filled island of Moskenesøy to the busy fishing town of Svolvaer. I've kayaked next to frolicking otters, wandered through meadows exploding with wildflowers, and marveled at the surreal sight of the midnight sun. I'm dying to return since Lofoten's enchantment keeps revealing new facets with every visit.

Reasons Why Your Next Adventure Should Be in Lofoten

Lofoten is not your usual vacation destination. It's a location that begs to be explored rather than only seen. Every nook in this place cries out for adventure. Climb to the summit of Ryten for breathtaking vistas that will blow your mind. Paddle a kayak across the glistening Trollfjorden, a breathtaking fjord defended by imposing rocks. Experience the cold waves of Unstad, a paradise for thrill-seekers. Alternatively, just stroll around a classic fishing town and take in the timeless beauty and sea air.

What This Handbook Provides

This book is your ticket to discovering Lofoten's mysteries. These pages include the following:

Detailed information on all the must-see attractions and hidden gems: I'll lead you to the experiences that will make your Lofoten journey memorable, from quaint villages and historical landmarks to breath-taking natural marvels and outdoor adventures.

A realistic guide to trip planning: I'll cover everything you need to know to ensure a hassle-free and pleasurable travel experience, including lodging, food, and transportation, whether you're on a tight budget or can afford to spend.

Insights into local culture and traditions: Develop a greater understanding of the distinctive way of living in this isolated island by learning about the lively culture and rich history of the Lofoten people. Suggested reading and undiscovered treasures: I'll share my finest locations, hidden trails, and insider knowledge as a seasoned Lofoten traveler to make sure you see all the islands have to offer.

Come with me to the Lofoten Islands, and together, let's make lifelong memories.

Brief History

Lofoten Islands: A Journey Through Time, Tradition, and Stunning Beauty

Imagine green peaks slicing the Arctic sky, turquoise fjords sculpted by ancient glaciers, and charming fishing communities perched on rugged coasts. Inhale the sea air, laced with the perfume of drying fish, and listen to the murmurs of a rich history dating back millennia. This is Lofoten, a Norwegian archipelago where time seems to pause and nature reigns supreme.

Echoes from the Past: Hunters to Vikings

The earliest echoes of human presence in Lofoten date back to the Stone Age, some 11,000 years ago. These early residents, expert hunters and gatherers, left their mark on the stunning terrain via rock sculptures and burial mounds. They became a nautical people throughout the ages, their lives determined by the rhythm of the tides and the riches of the ocean.

During the Viking Age, which lasted from the eighth to the eleventh century, Lofoten became a center of power and commerce. Håkon Jarl, a mythical chieftain, reigned from great longhouses with authority that extended beyond the islands. The Lofotr Viking Museum on Vestvågøya island is a replica of the world's biggest Viking longhouse, showcasing the era's architectural brilliance.

Cod and Commerce: The Rising of a Fishing Nation

The arrival of King Øystein in the 12th century marked a new era in Lofoten history. He founded Kabelvåg, the archipelago's first permanent town, and constructed a church to strengthen Christianity's presence on the islands. However, it was cod, the "silver of the sea," that actually molded Lofoten's fate.

From the Middle Ages on, the Lofoten fisheries became a pillar of the Norwegian economy. Every winter, hundreds of fishermen traveled to the islands, enticed by the prospect of a plentiful catch. The air was alive with activity as boats bobbed on the waves, nets snagged with gleaming fish, and settlements hummed with the energy of commerce and joy.

Stockfish, A Culinary Legacy

Lofoten's distinctive environment, with its chilly temperatures and constant winds, gave rise to a distinct culinary tradition: stockfish. This air-dried fish, a symbol of the islands' endurance and ingenuity, became a highly valued export across Europe. Even today, the sight of rows of stockfish drying on wooden racks is an iconic picture of Lofoten, their golden bodies swinging in the breeze like silent sentinels.

Modern Metamorphosis: From Fishing To Tourism

The twentieth century presented new problems. The collapse in cod stocks compelled Lofoten to diversify its economy. Tourism developed as a light of hope, and the islands' stunning scenery, attractive communities, and lively culture drew people from all over the world.

Today, Lofoten is a sanctuary for adventurers, nature enthusiasts, and photographers. Hikers climb towering peaks, kayakers negotiate mirror-like fjords, and surfers chase waves under the midnight sun. Foodies enjoy fresh seafood, while painters get inspiration from the ever-changing light and stunning landscape.

A Balancing Act: Preserving the Past while Embracing the Future

As tourism grows, Lofoten has the problem of maintaining its delicate equilibrium. The islands try to preserve their traditional way of life, respect for the natural environment, and distinct cultural identity. They greet guests with open arms, but warn them to tread lightly on this treasured country.

A Soulful Journey

Lofoten is more than simply a collection of islands; it's a real, breathing organism with a tale written in its mountains, spoken in the wind, and tasted in the sea salt. It's a location where history and nature coexist, where old traditions live on, and the spirit of adventure soars. So, if you want to take a voyage that will stir your spirit, where time stops still and nature reigns supreme, go no further than the Lofoten Islands.

TRAVEL PLANNING

To really enjoy your trip to the picturesque Lofoten Islands, you must prepare ahead of time. Whether you're a nature lover, an adventurer, or a cultural traveler, proper planning assures a smooth and enjoyable tour of this fascinating archipelago.

Best Time to Visit

Choosing the correct time to visit the Lofoten Islands is critical to experiencing the full range of its natural beauties and cultural experiences. Each season has its own attraction that appeals to various interests and inclinations. Here's a tip to help you decide on the optimum time for your visit:

Summer (June-August)

Midnight Sun Magic: Summer is known for the breathtaking Midnight Sun phenomena. The sun does not set for weeks, leaving the islands in a gentle, golden light. This season is perfect for hikers, outdoor lovers, and photographers, with more daylight hours for exploring.

Mild Temperatures: Enjoy temps between 10°C and 20°C (50°F to 68°F). It's the ideal season for kayaking, fishing, and exploring the many hiking paths without the cold of winter.

Vibrant Festivals: Summer provides exciting festivals and cultural activities. Visitors may immerse themselves in the colorful local culture by attending music festivals or participating in traditional ceremonies.

Autumn (September-November)

Golden Foliage: Experience the islands drenched in fall colors as the scenery turns into a tapestry of crimson, orange, and gold. This season is ideal for photographers, as they may capture the reflection of brilliant hues in the fjords.

Preview of the Northern Lights Although not as common as in winter, October brings the first sightings of the Northern Lights. Clear evenings provide possibilities to see auroras dancing across the black sky.

A quieter atmosphere: As the summer throngs depart, the mood will become more tranquil. It's an ideal time for people seeking a peaceful retreat among breathtaking landscapes.

Winter (December-February)

Aurora Borealis Spectacle: Winter is known with the breathtaking Northern Lights. The dark arctic nights provide a canvas for the dancing auroras, resulting in a spectacular display that draws aurora seekers from all over the globe.

Snow-Covered Landscapes: Lofoten is covered with snow, creating a winter paradise. Activities include winter dog sledding, snowshoeing, and skiing gain popularity, offering a new viewpoint on the islands' splendor.

Cozy atmosphere: Enjoy the pleasant atmosphere of winter in Lofoten. Snuggle up in traditional barbers, eat local food beside a warm fireplace, and soak in the island's beauty during the calmer off-season.

Spring (March-May)

Nature Rejuvenation: Spring delivers a slow thaw, transforming snow-covered landscapes into brilliant vegetation. Witness the islands come to life as flowers bloom and migratory birds return to their breeding places.

Increased Daylight: Longer days and more daylight make it an ideal time for a combination of winter and summer sports. It is a transitional stage that appeals to a wide range of interests.

The fishing season begins: Spring signals the start of the fishing season, providing an opportunity for angling lovers to participate in this traditional Lofoten sport.

Ultimately, the ideal season to visit Lofoten is determined by your choices, whether you like the boundless sunshine of summer, the mesmerizing Northern Lights of winter, or the quiet beauty of autumn and spring. Each season reveals a new aspect of Lofoten's charm, offering a unique and unforgettable experience for each visitor.

Packing Checklist

Lofoten Islands Packing List for Every Traveler

Traveling to the picturesque Lofoten Islands requires careful preparation to ensure you are well-prepared for the different scenery and activities on offer. Whether you're planning a weekend getaway, a 5-day excursion, or a 7-day expedition, here's a full packing list to make your trip smooth and pleasurable.

Weekend Escape (2-3 Day)

Clothes:

- Summer clothes should be lightweight and moisture-wicking, while insulating layers should be worn during the colder months.
- Waterproof and windproof jacket to guard against the island's unpredictable weather.
- Wear comfortable hiking boots or sturdy walking shoes.
- Swimsuit if you want to swim in the fjords or explore the sea.

Outdoor Equipment:

- Bring a daypack for hiking and exploring.
- Sunscreen and sunglasses for sunny days.
- A small umbrella or rain poncho for unexpected rainfall.
- Sun-protective hat or cap.

Electronics:

- Camera to capture magnificent vistas.
- Use a portable charger to keep your gadgets charged during outside activities.
- A travel adaptor for charging electrical gadgets.

Miscellaneous:

- Use a water bottle to remain hydrated.
- Snacks for energy when hiking.
- Toiletries in travel size.
- A lightweight, quick-dry towel.

Five-Day Adventure

Clothes:

- Expanded wardrobe to accommodate varied activities, ranging from casual attire for exploring to warmer layers for nights.
- Waterproof and insulated gloves for inclement weather.
- A combination of quick-drying and moisture-wicking clothing for variable weather situations.

Outdoor Equipment:

- A sturdy backpack with adequate room for longer trips.
- Binoculars for birding and admiring faraway views.
- For adaptability, choose a multitool or Swiss Army knife.
- Use a headlamp or flashlight for nighttime activities.

Electronics:

- Portable power bank with a larger capacity for extended usage.
- Use high-quality camera equipment to capture lengthy moments.
- A waterproof phone cover provides extra protection.

Miscellaneous:

- First aid kit with necessities.
- Maps and navigation aids for longer adventures.
- A reusable shopping bag for gathering local gems.

7-day exploration

Garments:

- Wide range of garments for diverse weather situations.
- Insulated, waterproof boots for longer walks.
- Additional pairs of socks and underpants.

Outdoor Gear:

- Bring camping equipment if staying outside overnight.
- A lightweight and tiny tent for camping expeditions.

- GPS gadget for tracking distant trails and places.

Electronics:
- A DSLR camera for high-quality photos.
- An international SIM card allows for expanded connection.
- Use a laptop or tablet for longer excursions.

Miscellaneous:
- Keep a travel diary to capture your longer vacation.
- Travel-sized washing detergent for extended visits.
- A portable water filter for isolated locations.

Budgeting Tips

Planning a vacation to these beautiful islands is thrilling, and staying within your budget may make the experience much more delightful. Here are some helpful budgeting suggestions to help you get the most out of your visit:

- **Accommodations:** Stay at traditional robbers or guesthouses for a genuine experience. Booking ahead of time might help you save money.

- **Meals:** Visit nearby markets for fresh vegetables and snacks. To keep your food expenditure in check, combine eating out with cooking at home.
- **transit:** Use public transit or carpool whenever feasible. It's not just cost-effective but also environmentally beneficial. Additionally, picturesque drives are part of the Lofoten experience!
- **Outdoor Activities:** Enjoy nature without spending too much money. Hiking routes, beaches, and vistas are often free. Bring a picnic and enjoy the gorgeous landscape.
- **Cultural Experiences:** Identify free or low-cost cultural events and festivals. Participating in local customs does not necessarily come at a high cost.
- **Shopping:** Choose locally created and affordable souvenirs to save money. Small, distinctive crafts often convey a more compelling tale than expensive items.
- **Tech and Connectivity:** Use free Wi-Fi at cafés and motels. Roaming expenses may mount up, so consider purchasing a local SIM card for your phone.
- Maintain a flexible itinerary to accommodate unexpected plans and possibilities. The finest experiences in

Lofoten are sometimes spontaneous, and they may even save you some money.

- **BYOB (Bring Your Own Basics):** Bring necessities such as reusable water bottles and thermos. It not only benefits the environment but also saves money on drink purchases.
- **Off-Peak Travel:** If your schedule permits, visit during shoulder seasons. You'll get better rates on lodgings, and the islands are just as beautiful with less people.
- **Cash Considerations:** While most locations take credit cards, it's recommended to bring cash for smaller shops and marketplaces.
- **Budget applications:** Use budgeting applications to monitor your expenditures. It's a simple method to keep track of your spending and prevent financial shocks.

Visa and travel requirements

You're in for a treat: craggy mountains, turquoise lakes, and picturesque fishing towns await. But, before you pack your warmest socks and go out to see the Northern Lights, let's go over the practicalities. Here's all you need know about visas and travel restrictions for your Lofoten adventure:

Visa

The good news is that Lofoten is part of Norway, which is part of the Schengen Zone. That means that if you are a citizen of a Schengen nation (which includes most European countries, the United States, Canada, Australia, and New Zealand), you may enter without a visa and remain for up to 90 days for tourism or business. There's no paperwork or worry, just you and the gorgeous surroundings.

Non-Schengen nationals face somewhat different circumstances. You'll need a Schengen visa to visit Norway and remain for your Lofoten holiday. Don't worry; the procedure is typically simple. Consult your local Norwegian embassy or consulate for particular criteria and application forms. They will walk you through the process, which often includes showing evidence of travel insurance, adequate finances, and your return airline ticket.

Travel Requirement

Norway removed all COVID-related entrance criteria on October 27, 2023. So, no need to bring PCR tests or immunization certificates—just your spirit of adventure and a camera to capture those spectacular vistas.

Of course, things might change, so always check the most recent official information before your trip. Here are some useful resources:

- Norway International Travel Information: [https://travel.state.gov/content/travel/en/traveladvisories/traveladvisories.html/].
- The Royal Norwegian Embassy in your country: [https://www.regjeringen.no/no/dep/ud/id833/].
- Visit Lofoten at: [https://visitlofoten.com/].

Travel Insurance

Lofoten Island, a Norwegian island covered in green peaks and turquoise fjords, entices with its natural beauty and adventure. But, before you lace up your hiking boots and go out to see the Northern Lights, think about getting travel insurance. It's like a mystical cloak, protecting you from unexpected catastrophes and ensuring that your Lofoten adventure goes well.

Why Travel Insurance for Lofoten?

While Norway has excellent healthcare, unforeseen circumstances may still disturb your vacation. Imagine:

Medical emergencies: Sudden sickness or injury might result in costly medical bills.

vacation cancellations: Flight difficulties, illness, or unanticipated events may compel you to cancel your vacation, incurring charges.

Travel disruptions: Missed connections, missing baggage, or equipment damage might delay your itinerary.

Emergency evacuation: Unexpected occurrences, such as natural catastrophes or medical issues, may need costly emergency evacuation.

Travel insurance reduces these dangers by offering financial protection and precious peace of mind. Let's look at the sorts of coverage you could want for your Lofoten adventure:

Essential Coverage:
- **Medical:** Includes emergency medical bills, hospitalization, and doctor consultations. Consider selecting a plan that provides enough coverage for probable high expenditures in Norway.
- **Trip cancellation:** Reimburses prepaid non-refundable charges such as airfare and lodging if you must cancel your trip for

covered reasons (e.g., sickness or natural catastrophes).

- **Travel disruption:** Includes expenditures incurred as a result of missed connections, delayed flights, or missing baggage. This may involve extra lodging, transportation, or replacement necessities.
- **Personal possessions:** Covers the loss, theft, or damage to your bags and personal things.

Additional Consideration:

- **Adventure activities:** Make sure your coverage covers activities such as skiing, kayaking, or hiking. Some regular plans may omit them.
- **Gadget coverage:** If you're carrying pricey photography equipment or gadgets, you should consider purchasing supplementary coverage for these items.
- **Emergency Evacuation:** This might be critical, particularly if you're traveling to distant places. Choose a strategy that includes emergency medical evacuation, if necessary.

The Cost of Travel Insurance for Lofoten:

The cost of travel insurance for Lofoten depends on numerous variables, including:

- Your trip duration: Longer journeys need more coverage, resulting in higher premiums.
- Your age and health: Younger travelers often pay less than older passengers, although pre-existing medical issues may boost the cost.
- Level of coverage: More comprehensive plans with larger coverage levels are naturally more expensive.
- The insurance provider: Different firms have different costs and coverage choices.

To get an accurate quotation, compare rates from many trustworthy travel insurance companies. Remember, the cheapest choice may not be the best; favor appropriate coverage above cost.

Finding the Right Policy:
- Read the small print: Thoroughly examine the policy language to determine what is covered and what is not. Pay special attention to activity restrictions and medical coverage limits.
- examine coverage options: Don't only look at the price; examine the amount of coverage provided by various plans. Choose

one that meets your individual demands and risk tolerance.

- Select a reliable provider: Choose a well-established travel insurance provider with a strong track record of customer care and claims management.

Additional Resource:

- Compare travel insurance websites: World Nomads: [https://www.worldnomads.com/] .
- Travel Insurance Direct: [https://www.travelinsurancedirect.com.au/travel-insurance-quote].
- Squaremouth,[https://www.squaremouth.com/].

GETTING THERE

Lofoten, an archipelago off Norway's northern coast, beckons with spectacular mountains, rough coasts, and quaint fishing communities. It's a world of opposites, where ancient Viking sagas murmur in the wind and contemporary experiences take place under the mystical glory of the Northern Lights. However, before you can immerse yourself in its allure, you must first arrive. This guide will reveal the many transportation alternatives available to you, allowing you to create the ideal Lofoten arrival tale.

Transportation Options

The Lofoten Islands, an archipelago wrapped in raw beauty, entices travelers with spectacular vistas and bustling fishing settlements. But how can you navigate its unusual terrain? Fear not, intrepid visitor, as this guide reveals your transit options.

Traveling By Air

Flying to Lofoten Island: An Air Travel Guide for Global Adventurers

Air travel to Lofoten often necessitates connecting via a gateway city in Norway. Here are the major options:

Gateway Cities:

Oslo, Norway (OSL): Oslo Gardermoen Airport is the largest hub, offering numerous connections to Lofoten via airlines like SAS Scandinavian Airlines,Norwegian Air, and Widerøe. Flight timings from large cities vary, but anticipate 2-4 hours to reach Oslo, followed by a connecting flight (1.2-2 hours) to Bodø, Evenes, or Svolvær in Lofoten. Prices vary depending on origin, season, and booking lead time, but average €100-€300+ for a one-way ticket (off-season).

Bodø, Norway (BOO): Bodø Airport offers direct flights from international hubs including London, Amsterdam, and Copenhagen. Widerøe and Norwegian Air fly these routes, with travel lengths varying from 2-4 hours. Connecting flights to Svolvær or Leknes in Lofoten take around 20-30 minutes and cost between €50-€200.

Evenes, Norway (EVE): Harstad/Narvik Airport is farther north, with fewer connections but perhaps lower tickets. Airlines that fly here include SAS and Norwegian Air. Consider an extra bus (3 hours) or boat (4 hours) journey to Lofoten from Evenes. Flights may begin at €150, but remember that ground transit adds time and complication.

Flying to Lofoten from Europe:

Flying is the quickest and most convenient method to get to Lofoten Island from Europe. However, the majority of large European cities do not have direct flights to Lofoten. You'll need to connect via a gateway city, such as Oslo, Bodø or Evenes.

Gateway cities:

Oslo, Norway: Oslo Gardermoen Airport (OSL) is Norway's biggest airport, with the most regular connections to Lofoten. Norwegian Air, Widerøe, and SAS provide flights from Oslo to Bodø, Evenes, or Svolvaer Airport (SVJ). The flight time from Oslo to Bodø is around 1 hour 20 minutes, whereas trips to Evenes or Svolvær take 1 hour 30 minutes to 2 hours. Prices for a one-way ticket start about €100 in the off-season and may reach €300 or more during the high season.

Bodø, Norway: Bodø Airport (BOO) is a viable choice for traveling to Lofoten. It offers links with various European cities, including London, Copenhagen, and Amsterdam. From Bodø, Widerøe offers connecting flights to Svolvær or Leknes Airport (LKN). The flight time from Bodø to Svolvær is roughly 30 minutes, while trips to Leknes take around 20 minutes. Prices for a one-way ticket start about €50 in the off-season and may reach €200 or more during the high season.

Evenes, Norway: Harstad/Narvik Airport (EVE) is situated on the mainland, about 170 kilometers from Svolvær. Although it has fewer connections than Oslo or Bodø, it may be a viable choice if travel prices are favorable. From Evenes, you may take the bus or boat to Lofoten. The bus trip takes around 3 hours, while the boat ride takes about 4 hours. Prices for flights to Evenes vary based on the starting city and season, but a one-way ticket will cost roughly €150 or more.

Airlines:

Several airlines provide flights to Lofoten from Europe, including:

- SAS Scandinavian Airlines
- Norwegian Air
- Widerøe
- KLM Royal Dutch Airlines
- Lufthansa
- Eurowings Discover offers seasonal flights from Frankfurt to Evenes.

Flight Time:

The flight time from Europe to Lofoten will vary based on your starting point and number of connections. Travel time from major European cities such as London, Paris, and Amsterdam may be between 4 and 8 hours.

Cost:
The cost of a flight to Lofoten varies depending on the airline, the time of year, and how far in advance you book. During the off-season, a one-way ticket would typically cost between €100 and €300, with higher prices during peak season.

Flying to Lofoten from UK

For travelers going from the United Kingdom, flight travel is the most effective and convenient method to reach this Nordic paradise. Let's consider your options:

Gateway Cities:
Your trip usually starts with a flight to a gateway city in Norway. The two primary contenders are:

Oslo, Norway : Oslo Gardermoen Airport (OSL) is the main airport for connecting to Lofoten with airlines such as SAS Scandinavian Airlines, Norwegian Air, and Widerøe. Flights from London normally take roughly 3 hours to reach Oslo, followed by a connecting flight to Bodø, Evenes, or Svolvaer, which adds anything between 1.2 and 2 hours. Expect a one-way ticket to cost between £120 and £350, depending on the season and airline.

Bodø, Norway: Bodø Airport (BOO) offers direct flights from many UK airports, including London Heathrow, Manchester, and Edinburgh, with carriers such as Widerøe and Norwegian Air. Flight times vary between 2.5 and 3.5 hours. Connecting flights to Svolvær or Leknes take around 20-30 minutes and cost around £50-£200.

Booking Websites and Air Travel Tips to Lofoten Island:

Booking sites:
- Skyscanner:(https://www.skyscanner.net/) Compares prices and routes across many airlines.
- Momondo: (https://www.momondo.com/) - Another flight aggregator that helps you locate bargains.
- Google flights:(https://www.google.com/flights) - A comprehensive search with customisable criteria (such as luggage fees).
- Airlines' websites: Check with airlines such as SAS, Norwegian Air, Widerøe, KLM, and Lufthansa for special routes and incentives.

Tip for Booking:
- Be flexible: Consider other travel dates and airports, particularly during high season (June-August).

- Book early: Airlines often announce bargains and special deals months in advance. Register for email notifications.
- Compare prices: Search for the cheapest bargains using aggregators and airline websites.
- Consider baggage fees: Checked luggage on budget flights may incur additional fees. Consider travel insurance to protect against unforeseen cancellations or delays.
- Consider traveling to a gateway city, such as Oslo or Bodø, and then connecting to Lofoten by boat or airplane.

Traveling By Sea

Getting to the Lofoten Islands by water is an incredible experience, with breathtaking views of the Norwegian coastline and the opportunity to see marine species such as whales and dolphins. Here's a guide for getting there from different countries:

From Mainland Norway:

Bodø: This is the most popular launching place for ferries to the Lofoten Islands. The Hurtigruten boat sails from Bergen and goes down the coast, making stops at many Lofoten ports. The trip takes around 34 hours and costs between €100 and €200. Bodø-Svolvær offers a speedier ferry from Bodø to

Moskenes, taking around 3-4 hours and costing €50-€100.

Stamsund: This is a tiny harbor on the western side of the Lofoten Islands. Bodø-Svolvær offers a ferry from Bodø to Stamsund that takes around 2.5 hours and costs between €50 and €100.

Moskenes: This is the southernmost port on the Lofoten Islands. Bodø-Svolvær og Lofoten Ferries provide a 3-4 hour boat ride from Bodø to Moskenes, costing between €30 and €50.

From different European countries:
Denmark: There are no direct ferries from Denmark to the Lofoten Islands. To reach the Lofoten Islands, take a ferry from Hirtshals, Denmark to Kristiansand, Norway, followed by a ferry from Bodø. The trek lasts roughly two days and costs about €200-€300.

Germany: There are no direct ferries from Germany to the Lofoten Islands. To reach the Lofoten Islands, take a ferry from Kiel, Germany to Oslo, Norway, then connect with another vessel from Bodø. The trip lasts roughly 2-3 days and costs about €300-€400.

United Kingdom: There are no direct ferries from the UK to the Lofoten Islands. However, you may take a ferry from Newcastle, UK to Bergen, Norway, and then transfer to a Hurtigruten ship to the Lofoten Islands. The trek takes roughly three to four days and costs between €400 and €500.

Where To Book:
You may buy your ferry tickets online at the following ferry operator websites:

- **Direct Ferries:**
  https://www.directferries.com/
- **AFerry:**
  https://www.aferry.co.uk/

Cost:
The cost of traveling to the Lofoten Islands by water varies according to the route, ferry operator, season, and kind of ticket. Expect to spend between €100 and €500 for a one-way journey.

Tips:
- Reserve your ferry tickets in advance, particularly during peak season (June-August).
- Consider purchasing a travel pass that covers ferry and other transportation in Norway.

- Even in the summer, the Lofoten Islands may be chilly and wet, so pack accordingly.
- If you are prone to seasickness, bring some medicine with you.

Moving Around

Lofoten is a wonderful vacation for nature lovers, photographers, and adventurers alike. However, for first-time tourists, traversing this island paradise might be a little intimidating. Fear not, intrepid traveler! This book will provide you with all of the information you need to navigate Lofoten smoothly and make the most of your vacation.

By Car Rental

However, getting about this archipelago paradise frequently needs wheels, which is where hiring a vehicle comes in. Buckle up, adventurer, as we dig into the world of Lofoten vehicle rentals, providing you with all of the information you need to travel these stunning coastlines with ease.

Where the rubber meets the road:

Major Players:

Avis: A worldwide company with offices at Moskenesøy (ferry terminal) and Leknes (Svolvaer Airport). Expect dependable transportation and multinational client service. Contact them at +47 76 95 00 00. Daily rates begin at around 800 NOK.

Budget: Another worldwide brand with a facility in Leknes (Svolvær Airport). Known for reasonable pricing and a diverse selection of vehicles. Call them at +47 76 95 00 40. Daily rates start at 600 NOK.

Europcar: Available at Leknes (Svolvær Airport) and Moskenesøy (ferry terminal). Provides luxury automobile alternatives with an emphasis on customer service. Contact them at +47 76 95 14 00. Daily rates begin at around 900 NOK.

Local Heroes: Do not underestimate the local players! They often provide individual attention, affordable pricing, and unique automobile alternatives. Consider Leknes Bilutleie (+47 76 96 14 10) and Lofoten Bilutleie (+47 76 95 14 50). Daily prices vary according to the automobile and season, but they should be similar to big brands.

Beyond the big names:
Lofoten Rent-A-Car: Specializes on used automobiles, providing affordable alternatives. Located at Moskenesøy (ferry terminal). Contact them at +47 95 78 31 60. Daily charges start at roughly 500 NOK.

Rent-A-Wreck Lofoten: If you're on a tight budget and don't mind a few bumps on the road, this firm sells older, less expensive vehicles. Located in Leknes. Contact them at +47 91 19 35 36. Daily charges begin at around 300 NOK.

Prices vary based on the season, automobile type, rental term, and optional extras such as insurance. Booking in advance, particularly during peak season (June-August), is strongly advised.

Setting Up for the Ride:

- Essentials: Bring your driver's license (if not EU-issued), credit card, and insurance documents.
- Know the Rules: Familiarize yourself with Norwegian traffic regulations, such as speed limits, right-of-way rules, and single-lane bridge etiquette.
- Fuel Up: Gas stations are widely distributed, so fill up anytime you find one, particularly in distant locations.
- Embrace the Adventure: Lofoten roads might be small and twisting, but the scenery is worth it! Enjoy the picturesque route and don't be scared to stop and discover unexpected treasures along the way.

- If you're coming in the cooler months (November-March), consider renting a vehicle with winter tires for increased safety on snowy or icy roads.

With the correct vehicle and a sense of adventure, you're ready to explore the Lofoten Islands. So, hit the throttle, take in the surroundings, and make memories that last a lifetime!

By Buses

Lofoten's beauty isn't only for those with cars. Public buses provide a cost-effective and picturesque way to visit the islands, immersing you in the local rhythm and breathtaking scenery. But don't worry; arranging your bus journey is simpler than negotiating a Lofoten fjord with a kayak.

Charting Your Course:
The primary bus network in Lofoten is run by Nordland County Council and serves most major cities and villages. There are two primary routes:

Route 170, Bodø-Ålesund: This route connects Bodø in mainland Norway to Moskenes and Reine in Lofoten via the E10 highway.

Lofoten Expressen (Route 300): This express bus travels from Narvik to Å, stopping in key cities such as Svolvaer and Leknes.

Find Your Ride:
- Website: The official Nordland County Council website (https://www.reisnordland.no/) has complete schedules, route maps, and ticket information.
- App: Get the Reis Nordland app for real-time bus monitoring, ticket buying, and personalized route planning.
- Tourist Information: Local tourist information centers provide printed schedules and may provide assistance.

Ticket Talk
- Ticket Prices: Fares vary based on distance traveled. Expect to spend between 50 and 100 NOK for shorter excursions and 150 to 200 NOK for longer trips.
- Buy a Ticket: Tickets may be paid on the bus with a debit or credit card (usually with a 20 NOK fee), online via the Reis Nordland app (discounted!), or at ticket machines at bus terminals.
- Travel Passes: for further savings and convenience, consider obtaining a travel

pass that allows you unlimited travel on buses and ferries for a certain length of time.

Tip for a Smooth Ride:
- Plan Ahead: Due to restricted schedules, particularly outside peak season, plan your excursions carefully and check timetables in advance.
- Be Flexible: Buses may operate slightly behind schedule, so allow for buffer time for connections and unexpected stops.
- Pack Essentials: Bring food, drink, and entertainment for longer trips. Remember that Lofoten's weather may be unpredictable, so prepare appropriately.
- Embrace the Experience: Sit back, relax, and enjoy the landscape! Public buses provide a unique opportunity to engage with local culture while also seeing Lofoten's ever-changing scenery.
- Consider combining bus and ferry trips to see more isolated islands and settlements. Take the boat from Bodø to Moskenes and then tour the islands via bus, stopping in Reine, Å, and Henningsvær.

By Taxi

Lofoten's appeal is shown not just along gorgeous roads and meandering bus routes, but also in the comfort and convenience of taxis. Whether you need a fast transport between villages, a door-to-door shuttle for your luggage-laden arrival, or a customized island excursion, taxis provide a flexible and stress-free way to see Lofoten's enchantment.

Flag Down a Fare:

Unlike in big cities, calling a cab on the street in Lofoten is uncommon. Here's how to secure your ride:

Taxi companies:

Several taxi companies operate in Lofoten, the most important of which are:

Vestvågøy Taxi: Leknes (+47 07550), Lokal Taxi Vågan (+47 07550), and Traveller Taxi (+47 90 90 91 90) provide service to Leknes, Svolvær, and nearby locations.

Moskenes Taxi: Moskenes (+47 97 11 85 77) serves the western Lofoten area.

Stamsund Taxi: Stamsund (+47 76 56 00 90) serves the eastern Lofoten Islands.

Booking In Advance:

Pre-booking your cab, particularly during peak season or for late-night arrivals, is strongly suggested. To make bookings, call your preferred firm directly or visit their websites (if accessible).

Private Taxi Hiring:

Hire a private cab for customized island exploration or multi-day vacations. Local businesses often combine guided tours with transportation, giving interesting commentary and insider information. Prices vary according to time, distance, and preferred itinerary.

Fair Play:

Taxi prices in Lofoten are computed using a meter system, which takes into account distance, time, and any tolls incurred. Expect to spend between 50 and 70 NOK each kilometer, plus an extra beginning cost. Tipping, although not required, is appreciated.

Apps and Online Bookings:
While less widespread than in bigger cities, some taxi firms provide online booking via their websites or third-party applications. Check with your selected provider for availability.

Insider Tip:
- Share a Ride: Consider splitting the cost of a cab with others.
- Compare Prices: Get quotations from many firms to obtain the best rate.
- Carry Cash: Although some cabs take credit cards, having cash on hand is usually recommended in rural places.
- Enjoy the Ride: Take in the beauty as your friendly taxi driver navigates the twisting roads.

By Ferry

The Lofoten Islands are a patchwork of stunning vistas, quaint communities, and hidden treasures dispersed across the Norwegian Sea. And what better way to link these active island strands than by boat, where you can take in the stunning coastline landscape and feel the beat of local life? This book will give you all the information you need to manage the Lofoten ferry system like a seasoned sailor.

Charting Your Course:

Several ferry lines traverse the Lofoten archipelago, each providing distinct experiences and connections. Here are the main players:

Bodø-Moskenes: This primary highway links the mainland town of Bodø to the western Lofoten island of Moskenes, which is the entryway to Reine and Å. It is operated by Torghatten Nord.

Moskenes-Bodø (via Værøy og Røst): This picturesque trip from Bodø to Moskenes includes stops at the isolated and bird-rich islands of Værøy and Røst. Book via Torghatten Nord.

Moskenes, Å-Svolvær, Stamsund: This route links important settlements in western and eastern

Lofoten, providing options for island hopping. Boreal is responsible for operation.

Hurtigruten: The renowned coastal cruise line makes stops in Lofoten, including Stamsund, Svolvær, and Stokmarknes, offering a unique mix of transportation and tourism.

Finding Your Ticket:
- Torghatten Nord: https://www.torghatten-nord.no/ (online booking available)
- Boreal: https://www.boreal.no/home/ (online booking available)
- Hurtigruten: https://www.hurtigruten.com/ (online booking available)

Fair Play:
Ferry fares vary according to route, distance, and passenger class (foot passenger, bike, automobile). Expect to pay about:

- Foot passenger: 50-150 NOK for shorter journeys, 200-300 NOK for longer travels.
- Car: 500-1000 NOK based on vehicle size and distance.
- Bicycle: 50–100 NOK.

Insider Tip:

- Book in advance: It is encouraged to reserve your space online, especially during peak season (June-August) and for automobile travel.
- Consider travel passes: The Lofoten Guest Card and Nordland Travel Card provide reduced ferry costs and other travel incentives.
- Priority is given to walk-on customers, so come early on shorter routes.
- Enjoy the onboard experience with cafés, shops, and observation decks for breathtaking views.
- Be flexible with scheduling: Weather might impact ferry schedules, so include a buffer time in your plan.
- Combining boats, buses, and taxis allows for smooth multi-island exploration. For example, take the boat from Bodø to Moskenes, tour Reine and Å by bus, then take the ferry to Stamsund and connect to Svolvær by cab.

ACCOMMODATIONS

Lofoten, with its spectacular scenery, quaint fishing communities, and dynamic culture, provides an unforgettable experience for every visitor. However, picking the correct accommodations may make or break your vacation. Fear not, explorer; this book will dig into all of the different alternatives Lofoten has to offer, helping you locate your ideal island sanctuary.

Luxury Hotels & Prices

Luxurious Lofoten: Four Dreamy Hotels for a Memorable Escape

Lofoten's untamed scenery and lovely communities entice vacationers looking for an out-of-the-ordinary retreat. However, for those who want a bit of luxury to their experience, the islands provide a range of exquisite hotels that combine contemporary comfort with spectacular nature. Buckle up, because we're plunging into the world of 4 top-notch Lofoten hotels that will pamper you on your island adventure:

1. Henningsvaer Rorbuer (A Historic Gem with Modern Touches): Consider staying in a historic building , thoroughly updated for maximum comfort. Henningsvær Rorbuer provides wonderfully refurbished fisherman's cottages with modern designs, soft furniture, and fully equipped kitchens. But the true star of the show is the scenery; walk outside your cabin and be captivated by the vibrant waterfront and majestic mountainscape. Amenities include private balconies with sea views, contemporary bathrooms with heated floors, fully fitted kitchens, complimentary Wi-Fi, laundry facilities, and an on-site restaurant and bar,price starting at 3,500 NOK per night.

Location: Henningsværvågen 32-34, 8300 Bodø, Norway, a charming fishing community famed for its colorful location on the water's edge.

Website: https://www.henningsvar-rorbuer.no/en/

Phone Number: +47 76 05 12 88

Best Route: Fly into Evenes Airport (Harstad/Narvik) and take a 2-hour scenic drive or a 30-minute ferry journey from Bodø to reach Henningsvær.

2. Svolvær Guesthouse (Boutique Charm in the Heart of the City): Svolvær Guesthouse offers a sophisticated and private atmosphere. This wonderfully renovated 19th-century building oozes warmth and charm, with uniquely designed rooms that include elegant décor and modern facilities. Enjoy wonderful breakfasts created with local products on the rooftop patio, which offers panoramic views of the town and surrounding mountains. Amenities include Individually furnished rooms with distinct appeal, comfy mattresses with down duvets, contemporary bathrooms with rain showers, complimentary breakfast, a rooftop terrace with panoramic views, and free WiFi,price start at 2,800 NOK/night.

Location: Strandgata 25, 8300 Svolvær, Norway. Svolvær is the busy capital of Lofoten, with convenient access to shopping, restaurants, and cultural activities.

Website:
https://www.tripadvisor.com/Hotels-g227941-Svolvaer_Vagan_Lofoten_Islands_Nordland_Northern_Norway-Hotels.html

Phone Number: +47 90 09 99 69

Best Route: Fly into Evenes Airport (Harstad/Narvik) and take a 1.5-hour scenic drive or a 45-minute boat journey from Bodø to Svolvær.

3. The Egg Hotel (Modern Luxury Meets Nature): The Egg Hotel raises the bar for luxurious lodgings. These distinctive egg-shaped houses located on the hillside provide amazing vistas and a fully immersive encounter with nature. Each "egg" has a comfortable double bed, a bathroom with a shower, and a private patio ideal for stargazing beneath the midnight sun or the Northern Lights. Amenities include a private egg-shaped room with breathtaking views, a comfortable double bed, a contemporary bathroom with a shower, a private patio, free Wi-Fi, and access to the communal lounge and sauna,prices start from 4,200 NOK per night.

Location: Henningsvær Storvagan 87, 8300 Bodø, Norway,affording spectacular views of the surrounding mountains and the Norwegian Sea.

Website:
https://www.firsthotels.com/hotels/norway/lofoten/.
Phone Number: +47 91 75 10 30

Best Route: Fly into Evenes Airport (Harstad/Narvik) and take a 2-hour scenic drive or a

30-minute ferry journey from Bodø to reach Henningsvær.

4. Eliassen Rorbuer & Hotel (Rustic Luxury with a View): Eliassen Rorbuer & Hotel combines the beauty of traditional with contemporary amenities and breathtaking sea views. Choose from attractively appointed rooms with private balconies and a modern hotel room with a minimalist style. In the evening, unwind at the hotel. Amenities include traditional with private balconies and modern hotel rooms, fully equipped kitchens (in), comfortable beds with down duvets, modern bathrooms with rain showers, complimentary breakfast, on-site restaurant serving local specialties, spa facilities with sauna and hot tub, and free Wi-Fi,price starting at 3,200 NOK per night.

Location: 8360 Fredvang, Norway. Fredvang is a little fishing community that provides a genuine Lofoten experience away from the throng.

Website: https://rorbuer.no/

Phone Number: +47 76 04 12 22

The Best Route: From Evenes Airport (Harstad/Narvik), Moskenes is a 2-hour picturesque drive or 30-minute boat journey from Bodø. From there, Fredvang is a 45-minute drive away.

Bread and Breakfast

Lofoten's enchantment is not limited to big hotels; it also includes the warmth and local character of bed and breakfasts (B&Bs). These cozy havens provide an authentic experience, connecting you with the islands' rich culture and breathtaking surroundings. So, gather your spirit of adventure, and prepare to explore these hidden gems:

1. Sakrisøy Gjestegard: Step back in time at this old farmhouse B&B, which has been lovingly refurbished and provides a look into traditional Lofoten life. It emanates tranquility since it is surrounded by undulating hills and sheep pastures. Amenities include a communal kitchen, garden patio, common room with fireplace, Wi-Fi, and free parking. Prices start at 1,200 NOK per night for a double room with shared bathroom,Open year round. Phone number: +47 95 25 09 30.

- **Location:** Sakrisøy Veien 56, 8390 Leknes, Norway.

- **Website:** [https://www.sakrisoy.no/]

- **Best Route:** Fly at Evenes Airport (Harstad/Narvik) and take a 1-hour scenic drive or a 30-minute ferry journey from Bodø to Leknes. Sakrisøy is about a 15-minute drive from there.

2. Nyvågar Rorbu Hotell: This quaint bed and breakfast offers a traditional lifestyle. Choose between historic red cabins and contemporary flats, each with spectacular sea views and comfy facilities. Enjoy the tranquil setting and closeness to the lively fishing community of Nyvågar. Amenities include private kitchens (in most rooms), laundry facilities, Wi-Fi, free parking, on-site restaurant (seasonal). Price Starts at 1,500 NOK per night (with shared bathroom). Phone Number: +47 76 07 87 40, open year round.

- **Location:** Nyvågarvågen 80, 8300 Bodø, Norway.

- **Best Route:** Fly to Bodø Airport and take a cab or bus to Nyvågar (15-minute ride).

3. Reine Rorbuer: Located in the charming hamlet of Reine, famed for its dramatic surroundings and colorful port, this B&B provides classic with a contemporary touch. Each cabin has a distinct personality and spectacular fjord views, ensuring an unforgettable visit. Amenities include private kitchens (in most rooms), Wi-Fi, free parking, and laundry facilities (surcharge). Price Starts at 1,800 NOK per night for a room with a shared bathroom. Phone number: +47 91 75 52 40,Open/closed hours are April-October.

- **Moskenesøy** Veien 226, 8387 Reine, Norway.

- Website:[https://www.reinerorbuer.no/]

- **The Best Route:** From Evenes Airport (Harstad/Narvik), Moskenes is a 2-hour picturesque drive or 30-minute boat journey from Bodø. From there, Reine is a 45-minute drive away.

Camping Options

Lofoten's raw beauty is best experienced while immersed in its natural settings. What better way to enjoy it than to camp beneath the midnight sun or the Northern Lights? Here are three different camping choices to inspire your adventure:

1. Moskenes Camping: Enjoy the authentic Lofoten experience at our family-run campground, located among majestic mountains and facing the spectacular Moskenesstraumen tidal current. For a hint of glamping, choose between tent pitches, campervan spaces, and comfortable camping pods. Amenities include shared kitchen, laundry room, baths, Wi-Fi (limited), playground, kayak and bike rentals, on-site café, and grocery store. Price tent pitches start at 250 NOK per night (depending on the season and size), campervan pitches at 350 NOK per night, and camping pods at 600 NOK per night,Phone number: +47 91 59 08 78.

- Moskenesøy Veien 816, 8340 Reine, Norway.

- Opening/Closing Hours: Open May through September.

- Site:[https://www.moskenescamping.no/]

- The Best Route: From Evenes Airport (Harstad/Narvik), Moskenes is a 2-hour picturesque drive or 30-minute boat journey from Bodø. The campground is conveniently positioned in the village.

2. Henningsvaer Camping: Experience the active village life of Henningsvær at our centrally situated campground. Enjoy spectacular harbor views and easy access to shopping, restaurants, and cultural activities. Enjoy the social environment and closeness to outdoor activities. Amenities include shared kitchen, baths, laundry room, Wi-Fi (limited), playground, bike rental, and walking distance to stores and restaurants. Price tent pitches start at 200 NOK per night (depending on the season and size), while campervan pitches start at 300 NOK per night.

- Location: Henningsvær Vågan 30, 8300 Bodø, Norway.

- Opening/Closing Hours: Open June through August.

- Phone Number: +47 47 48 23 33.

- The Best Route: Fly into Evenes Airport (Harstad/Narvik) and take a 2-hour scenic drive or a 30-minute boat journey from Bodø to reach Henningsvær. The campground is only a short walk from the boat station.

3. **Kvalvika Beach:** Enjoy the wild Atlantic atmosphere at this lonely and stunning beach camping, which can only be reached by foot or boat. Hike through breathtaking countryside to find

this hidden treasure, ideal for experienced campers seeking seclusion and a connection with nature.

- Amenities: None (bring everything you need), with minimal cell network connectivity.

- Price: Free camping (a permit is necessary during high season).

- Location: Kvalvika Beach, 8330 Reine, Norway.

- Opening/closing hours: We are open year-round (weather permitting).

- Phone Number: N/A (permission information is accessible on the webpage linked below).

- Website: https://www.ut.no/

- The Best Route: Fly at Evenes Airport (Harstad/Narvik) and take a 2-hour scenic drive or a 30-minute ferry journey from Bodø to Reine. From Reine, you may trek the 4km route to Kvalvika Beach or join a local boat excursion (availability varies).

EXPLORING THE ISLANDS

Every explorer is captivated by the Lofoten Islands, which have craggy peaks, blue lakes, and lovely fishing settlements. But where do you start when there is so much to explore? This book goes into the heart of Lofoten, delivering insights into each island's distinct personality and must-see activities.

Popular Attractions

Lofoten's rocky beauty is not limited to experienced travelers. The islands are a treasure trove of safe and breathtaking attractions, providing a wonderful experience for all sorts of visitors. So, pack your luggage, bring your curiosity, and let's explore:

Reinebringen

This famous mountain, which rises 448 meters above Reinefjorden, rewards your efforts with panoramic views of colorful cottages, spectacular peaks, and the great ocean. Reinebringen's trail was developed naturally over millions of years as residents traveled its slopes for millennia.

Safety: While the trek is relatively difficult, proper footwear, hydration, and attention to weather conditions assure a safe excursion. Designated pathways make navigating simpler.

Activities: Hike to the peak for beautiful views, take great photographs, or have a picnic with a spectacular setting.

Best Time to Visit: Summer provides moderate temperatures and extended daylight hours, while autumn's colorful foliage is equally magnificent.

Entrance Fees: Free to hike; parking fees may apply near Reine.

Location: Reinebringen, 8396 Moskenes, Norway. Accessible by car or hiking trail from Reine village.

Opening Hours: Always accessible (weather permitting).

Entry Requirements: Good physical fitness and appropriate clothing.

HenningSvær

This charming community, dubbed the "Venice of Lofoten," has colorful waterfront homes, art galleries, and a lively atmosphere. Henningsvær, a centuries-old fishing community, prospered owing to its strategic position and plentiful cod stocks. There are no requirements for entry.

Safety: The village is pedestrian-friendly with designated sidewalks and well-maintained roads.

Activities: Visit art galleries, kayak around the harbor, hire bikes to explore the surroundings, or just enjoy the pleasant environment.

Best time to visit: Summer brings vibrant events and festivals, whilst spring and fall provide cooler weather and less people.

Entrance costs: Free to tour the village; specific costs apply for activities such as kayaking or gallery visits.

Location: Henningsvær, 8300 Bodø, Norway. Accessible by vehicle or boat from Bodø or Moskenes.

Opening Hours: Shops and restaurants normally open from 10:00-18:00.

Kabelvåg

Svolvær's attractive neighbor features historical landmarks, museums, and a dynamic port scene. Kabelvåg was established as a trade station centuries ago and played a key part in Lofoten's fishing economy. There are no entry requirements.

Safety: The town is walkable with designated pedestrian zones and well-lit streets.

Activities: Visit the Lofoten Stockfish Museum, admire traditional boats in the port, eat fresh seafood in eateries, or take a historical walking tour.

Best time to visit: Summer brings longer daylight hours and outdoor festivities, whilst winter brings the Aurora Borealis and less tourists.

Entrance Fees: Museums and activities charge varying fees; exploring the town is free.

Location: Kabelvåg, 8300 Bodø, Norway. Accessible by vehicle or boat from Bodø or Moskenes.

Opening Hours: Shops and restaurants normally open from 10:00-18:00. Museums have defined operating hours.

Nusfjord

This unusual fishing community, only accessible by foot or boat, provides a look into traditional Lofoten life. Established centuries ago, Nusfjord has remained mostly unaltered, showing traditional fishing (рыбацкие хижины) and fishing traditions.

Safety: The restricted automobile access and pedestrian-friendly routes foster a safe environment. Guided tours provide extra information and help.

Activities: Explore the historic , explore artisan stores and galleries, eat lunch at a traditional restaurant, or embark on a boat cruise for spectacular fjord views.

Best Time to Visit: Summer provides moderate temperatures and extended daylight hours, while spring and fall provide a more peaceful experience.

Entrance Fees: Museums and activities charge varying fees; exploring the village is free.

Location: Nusfjord, 8360 Bøstad, Norway. Accessible via boat from Reine or by foot from Nusfjord Camping.

Kvalvika Beach

This quiet beach has immaculate white sand, turquoise seas, and spectacular mountain backgrounds, providing a bit of heaven. Kvalvika's natural beauty has been concealed for millennia, drawing daring beach lovers in recent years.

Safety: Swim with caution due to strong currents. The walk may be strenuous, requiring suitable footwear and consideration to weather conditions.

Activities: Relax on the beach, swim in the cool waters (weather permitting), explore the gorgeous paths that encircle the beach, or have a picnic with spectacular views.

Best Time to Visit: Summer brings higher water temperatures, but spring and fall provide less visitors and maybe calmer waters.

Entrance Fees: Free to access the beach; parking fees may apply near the trailhead.

Location: Kvalvika Beach, 8396 Moskenes, Norway. Accessible by a 4km hike from Reine village or by boat tour.
Opening Hours: Always accessible (weather permitting).

Entry Requirements: Good physical fitness for the hike and appropriate clothing for the weather.

Lofoten

This unusual art gallery, situated in a traditional fishing cottage near Nusfjord, shows the works of famous Lofoten artist Gunnar Berg, known for his magnificent landscape paintings.

Berg established the gallery in 1991, and it provides a look into his creative vision as well as the beauty of Lofoten. There are no entry requirements.

Safety: The gallery is readily accessible and well-kept.

Activities: Explore the gallery's collection, learn about Berg's creative path, and shop for one-of-a-kind gifts.

Best Time to Visit: Open year-round, although summer provides longer hours and maybe more exhibits.

Entrance Fees: Vary according on season and exhibitions; check website for current information.

Location: Nusfjord, 8360 Bøstad, Norway. Accessible by boat from Reine or by foot from Nusfjord Camping.

Opening Hours: Seasonal; visit the website for updated information.

Hidden Gems

Exploring Lofoten's Hidden Gems: Beyond the Tourist Trail

Many people are drawn to Lofoten's spectacular scenery and attractive settlements, but genuine explorers want to go beyond the well-trodden trails. So, leave the masses behind and go out to find Lofoten's hidden gems:

Unstad Beach

This surfer's paradise has immaculate white beach, tremendous waves, and a rocky shoreline. Watch surfers dance with the water or just relax on the beach with stunning views.

Location: Flakstadøy island, accessible by car or bus from Leknes.

Uniqueness: Renowned surfing destination with breathtaking natural beauty and fewer crowds. **Activities:** Surfing, swimming, sunbathing, hiking, horseback riding.

Best Time to Visit: Summer for calmer waters and surfing; fall for fewer crowds and colorful foliage.

Munkebu Lighthouse

Perched on a stunning cliff edge, this 19th-century lighthouse provides panoramic views of the Moskenesstraumen tidal stream and its surrounding islands.

Location: Moskenesøy island, reachable by a 4km trek from Sørvågen.

Uniqueness: Stunning panoramas, historic lighthouse, and a feeling of isolation.

Activities: Hiking, photography, and lighthouse tours (summer).

The Best Time to Visit: Summer for longer daylight hours and warmer temperatures; winter for stunning seascapes and the possibility of seeing the Northern Lights.

Eggum

This abandoned fishing community, only accessible by boat or foot, provides a look into Lofoten's history. Explore the rustic рыбацкие хижины (fishing), envision the life of previous people, and enjoy the calm.

Location: Flakstadøy island, accessible by boat tour from Nusfjord or a challenging hike from Fredvang.

Uniqueness: Off-the-beaten-path experience, historical ambiance, serene atmosphere.

Activities: Hiking, exploring abandoned cabins, photography, kayaking.

Best Time to Visit: Summer for calmer waters and longer daylight hours; spring and autumn for fewer crowds and potential wildflowers.

Gimsøy Sand Dunes

This one-of-a-kind environment contains golden sand dunes rising from the shore, creating a strange desert-like atmosphere among the majestic mountains.

Location: Moskenesøy island, accessible by car or bus from Moskenes.

Uniqueness: Unique natural phenomenon, beautiful photo opportunities, peaceful environment.

Activities: Walking, sandboarding, exploring the dunes, picnicking.

Best Time to Visit: Summer for warmer temperatures and longer daylight hours; spring and autumn for fewer crowds and quieter weather.

Henningsvaer Football Field

This renowned football field, located on a tiny islet linked to Henningsvær by a bridge, provides breathtaking vistas and a unique athletic experience.

Location: Henningsvær settlement på Vestvågøy island.

Uniqueness: Picturesque setting, opportunity to play on a unique field, charming village atmosphere.

Activities: Playing football, enjoying the views, and exploring Henningsvær village.

Best Time to Visit: Summer for milder temperatures and longer daylight hours; winter for a chance to play under the Northern Lights (weather permitting).

OUTDOOR ACTIVITIES

The beauty of lofoten is more than just a feast for the eyes; it's an invitation to thrilling outdoor experiences! Whether you're an experienced traveler or a first-time visitor, the islands provide something for everyone. So, lace up your hiking boots, grab your sense of awe, and let's explore.

Hiking Trails

The Lofoten Islands, with their rugged peaks, turquoise seas, and picturesque fishing communities, are an outdoor enthusiast's heaven. Hiking routes wind across stunning terrain, providing panoramic views, secluded beaches, and interactions with various species. Whether you're a seasoned trekker or a casual traveler, Lofoten has a route waiting to be discovered. But, with so many alternatives, where do you start?

Safety First:
Safety is the most important consideration while hitting the trails. Here are some important considerations to bear in mind:

Choose the Right Trail: Match your fitness level and hiking experience to the trail's difficulty.

Choose well-marked and maintained paths, particularly if you're new to the region.

Check the weather conditions: Lofoten's weather may be unpredictable. Always check the weather before beginning your trek, and be prepared for changes. Pack the necessary clothes and accessories, such as strong hiking boots, waterproof layers, and a map.

Be alert of your surroundings: Look out for loose rocks, uneven ground, and unexpected drop-offs. When hiking near water, follow tide tables and leave no trace. Respect the environment by packing out rubbish and not disturbing animals or flora.

The Best Safe Places to Hike

Now, let's look at some of the greatest safe and engaging hiking paths Lofoten has to offer:

1. Reinebringen: This renowned climb offers spectacular panoramic views of Reinefjorden, colorful cottages, and towering mountain ranges. The fairly difficult trek takes around 2-3 hours to complete (round trip). Located in Reine, Moskenesøy island. Accessible by driving or walking from Reine village. The trailhead is clearly indicated.

Opening/closing hours: N/A (public path open year-round). However, in the winter or during storms, the walk might be dangerous.

2. Ryten, Kvalvika Beach: Hike up steep cliffs, taking in amazing views of the Moskstraumen maelstrom before descending to the remote and picturesque Kvalvika Beach. This fairly hard trek takes around 4-6 hours to complete (round trip). Located in Fredvang, Moskenesøy island. To get there take the boat from Renne to Kjerkefjorden or Vindstad and follow the signposted route from Fredvang.

Opening/closing hours: N/A (public path open year-round). However, in the winter or during storms, the walk might be dangerous.

3. Munkebu Lighthouse: Hike to a historic lighthouse positioned on a steep cliff edge, which provides beautiful sea views and a feeling of remoteness. This tough trek takes around 4-5 hours to complete (round trip). Located in Sørvågen, Moskenesøy island. Drive or take a bus from Sørvågen hamlet and follow the indicated route.
Opening/closing hours: N/A (public path open year-round). However, in the winter or during storms, the walk might be dangerous.

4. Henningsvaer Rundt (Around Henningsvær):
Take a picturesque stroll around the lovely port and majestic shoreline of Henningsvær town. This simple trek takes around 1-2 hours to complete and has great vistas. Located in Henningsvær, Vestvågøy island. Arrive by vehicle, bus, or boat from Bodø or Moskenes. The walk begins in the middle of the hamlet.

Opening/closing hours: N/A (public path open year-round).

Site: For more information about Henningsvær Tourism, see
[https://nerdnomads.com/henningsvaer-guide-lofoten].

With adequate preparation and a feeling of adventure, Lofoten's hiking paths provide amazing experiences in stunning scenery. Lace up your boots, take a deep breath of fresh air, and step by step experience the enchantment of Lofoten!

Water Activities

The Lofoten Islands, with their jagged coasts, crystal-clear seas, and abundant marine life, are ideal for water enthusiasts. The choices range from kayaking through peaceful fjords to surfing strong waves. Whether you're an experienced explorer or a first-time paddler, Lofoten offers an activity that will make your vacation unique.

1. Kayaking: Discover secret coves, traverse lovely bays, and appreciate Lofoten's beauty from a different angle. Kayaking is a peaceful and accessible sport suitable for families and groups.

Location: Several companies provide excursions and rentals across Lofoten. Popular beginning sites include Reine, Henningsvaer, Kabelvåg, and Moskenes.

Opening/closing hours: varies based on the operator. The majority operate throughout the summer months (May-September), with a few giving limited trips in the spring and fall.

Website and Phone Number:
Lofoten Adventures:
[https://lofotentours.com/tour/lofoten-in-winter-copy], +47 91 75 22 66

The Lofoten Kayak School:
[https://europeansmallislands.com/2016/12/04/small-island-schools-perform-well/],+ 47 94 83 65 10.

Reinebringen Kayak & Hiking:
[https://www.fjordtours.com/things-to-do-in-norway/kayaking/reine-lofoten/], +47 90 09 24 84

Entry requirements: Some operators need advance reservations, particularly during high season. Life jackets and basic paddling instructions are frequently provided.

2. Stand-up Paddleboarding (SUP): Glide at your own speed through peaceful coves and fjords, taking in the serenity and breathtaking views. SUP is a beginner-friendly activity that provides a new way to interact with water.

Location: Similar to kayaking, numerous companies provide SUP rentals and trips across Lofoten. Popular locations include Kabelvåg, Henningsvær, and Kvalvika Beach.

Opening/closing hours: varies based on the operator. Most operate throughout the summer months (May to September), with others giving limited rentals in the spring and fall.

Website and Phone Number:
Lofoten Aktiv: [https://www.lofoten-aktiv.no/en/], +47 90 19 52 95.

Lofoten Sea Adventures:
[https://adventure.norrona.com/en/northern-norway/winter-adventure-in-lofoten?utm_source=visitnorway&utm_medium=link]. +47 91 50 57 67

Lofoten Islands Kayak & SUP School:
[https://www.northadviser.com/activities-and-tours/kayak-course-lofoten/], +47 95 92 52 34.

Entry requirements: Most operators provide boards and paddles. During the high season, prior booking may be necessary.

3. Boat Tours: Take a guided boat excursion to discover secret bays, see animals such as sea eagles and humpback whales, and see Lofoten's majestic coastline from a new viewpoint.

Location: Tours leave from many ports in Lofoten, including Reine, Henningsvær, Moskenes, and Kabelvåg.

Opening/closing times: vary based on the operator and trip type. Most trips run throughout the summer months (May-September), with others giving limited alternatives in the spring and fall.

Website and phone number:
Hurtigruten Svalbarden:
https://www.hurtigrutensvalbard.com/, +47 79 02 61 00.

Reinebringen Kayak & Hiking: +47 90 09 24 84

Lofoten Adventures:
[https://lofotentours.com/], +47 91 75 22 66.

Entry criteria vary every trip. Some demand reservations in advance, particularly during high season. Dress warmly and comfortably, and wear appropriate boat deck footwear.

4. Fishing: On a guided fishing excursion, you may experience the excitement of reeling in cod, haddock, or even whales (ethically and within limits). Enjoy the fresh air, beautiful view, and wonderful reward!

Location: Several companies provide guided fishing expeditions from several ports in Lofoten. Popular destinations include Reine, Henningsvær, Moskenes, and Å.

Opening/closing hours: These vary based on the operator and the season. Most operate throughout the spring, summer, and early fall.

Phone Number:
Lofoten Havfiske: +47 91 56 11 24.

Kontakt Reinebringen Sjømat & Havfiske på +47 45 86 73 24.

Moskenes Øyhopping: +47 90 04 01 50.

Entry requirements: Most operators supply all required equipment and education. It is advised that you book in advance. Licenses may be necessary for some forms of fishing.

5. Surfing: Lofoten's Unstad Beach, regarded as Europe's Hawaii, provides tough waves and magnificent scenery for expert surfers. Lessons and rentals are provided for both beginners and intermediates.

Location: Unstad Beach, Flakstadøy Island.

Opening/closing hours: Surf conditions are ideal in the autumn and winter, although lessons and rentals may be offered during other seasons, depending on the operator.

Phone Number:

Lofoten Surfing: +47 90 15 55 60.

Unstad Arctic Surf: +47 76 04 44 00.

Entry Requirements: Independent surfing requires advanced abilities and the accompanying equipment. Lessons are strongly recommended for both beginners and intermediates.

Wildlife Encounters

The Lofoten Islands are more than simply magnificent vistas; they are also home to a rich range of fauna that awaits discovery. Meeting soaring sea eagles, lively otters, and beautiful whales may make your vacation memorable. Here's your guide to exploring Lofoten's wild side.

1. Sea Eagles: Watch these majestic birds of prey effortlessly glide across the sky.

Location: Found across the archipelago, particularly along coasts and cliffs.

How to get there: Travel by boat, kayak, or coastal walk. Join guided wildlife trips to get professional insights and boost your chances of seeing animals.

Entry requirements: There are no particular permits required for general wildlife observation. Respect their environment and keep a safe distance.

Opening/closing hours: N/A. Active throughout the day, however most sightings occur in the early mornings and nights.

2 Seals: Watch these lively critters laze on rocks or swim in the crystal-clear waters.

Location: Found on coasts, beaches, and skerries. Popular destinations include Eggum, Yttersand, and Vaerøy island. Accessible by vehicle, boat, or hiking routes. Kayaking provides a distinct viewpoint.

Entry requirements: None for responsible watching in public places. Please keep a safe distance and avoid upsetting them.

Opening/closing hours: N/A. Active all day, however tides sometimes obscure their visibility on rocks.

3. Whales: Behold the breathtaking sight of humpback whales breaching or pods gently gliding.

Location: Mostly in offshore seas around Andøya, Vesterålen, and Lofoten. Dedicated whale viewing trips leave from many ports.

How to Get There: Participate on a guided whale-watching trip. Whale-watching boats increase your chances of seeing whales.

Entry Requirements: Most trips adhere to appropriate whale-watching procedures. Follow the guide's recommendations and keep a polite distance.

Opening and closing hours: Tours are normally offered between May and September, when whales migrate through the region.

Entry fees: Fees for whale watching cruises vary based on the length and provider. Book in advance, particularly during the high season.

4 Puffins: During the spring and summer, look for these lovely seabirds with bright beaks breeding on cliff cliffs.

Location: Puffin colonies include Gimsøy, Røst, and Værøy Islands.

How to get there: Boat cruises intended for puffin viewing are offered. Alternatively, walk paths provide access to certain colonies.

Entry Requirements: Respect designated viewing areas and keep a safe distance to prevent upsetting birds.

Opening/Closing Times: Puffins arrive in colonies around April and leave in August or September. The ideal time to see them is during their mating season (May to July).

Entrance fees: Some puffin colonies or boat cruises may charge an admission fee. Check with the particular operators.

5 Otters: Find these lovely creatures swimming or frolicking near the shore.

Location: Mostly on rocky coastlines and skerries, with kelp forests. Nusfjord, Henningsvær, and Reine are prime spots for sightings.

How to get there: Travel by boat, kayak, or hiking along coastal paths. When seeing otters from public locations, use a calm approach and be patient since they are timid animals. There are no entry restrictions. Keep a safe distance and avoid upsetting them.

Opening/Closing hours: Wildlife is most active at dawn and dusk, although sightings may occur throughout the day.

Tips:
- Prioritize ethical and responsible wildlife viewing by respecting their habitat, maintaining a safe distance, and avoiding disturbing them.
- Dress appropriately for weather conditions. Lofoten's weather can be unpredictable, so wear layers and waterproof clothing.
- Pack essentials for outdoor activities, such as binoculars, a camera, and a guidebook.
- Consider guided excursions for greater sightings and expert insights.
- Follow legislation and local standards. Some regions may have limits on animal watching.

CULTURAL EXPERIENCES

Lofoten Islands are more than simply breathtaking vistas; they are also home to a distinct and lively culture that awaits exploration. From old Viking sagas to thriving fishing practices and modern art, immersing yourself in Lofoten's cultural tapestry will enhance your journey beyond measure.

Museums and Art Galleries

Introducing Lofoten's Artistic Soul: Museums and Art Galleries

Beyond its magnificent vistas and appealing animals, the Lofoten Islands have a thriving art scene that is firmly ingrained in their culture. Prepare to be captivated by its numerous creative manifestations, which range from rural seaside towns converted into artist centers to historical museums whispering Viking legendary stories. Let's take a voyage around some of the must-see museums and art galleries:

Lofotr Viking Museum (Borg): Step back in time to Borg, the biggest chieftain's home unearthed in Norway. Explore rebuilt houses, see traditional craft demonstrations, and immerse yourself in the lives of the Vikings who once inhabited these territories.

Located in Borg, Vestvågøy. An admission charge applies.

Opening/Closing times: May-September: 10:00 AM - 6:00 PM, Rest of the year: Tuesday-Friday 10:00 AM - 4:00 PM, Weekends 12:00 PM - 4:00 PM.

Getting there: The museum is accessible by automobile via the E10 highway towards Borg. There is parking accessible at the museum.

Public transportation: From Leknes Airport, take bus 180 to Borg. The bus station is about a 10-minute walk from the museum.

Website: https://www.lofotr.no/en/lofotr-vikingmuseum/

Museum Nordland (Bodø): Explore Lofoten's cultural heritage, including Stone Age tools, Viking artifacts, and traditional fishing equipment. Located in Sjøgata 2, 8000 Bodø. An admission charge is required.

Opening/Closing hours: Tuesday-Friday 11:00 AM - 5:00 PM, Saturday & Sunday 12:00 PM - 5:00 PM. Closed on Mondays.

The museum is conveniently placed in Bodø's city center, accessible by foot, bike, or public transit.

From Bodø Airport, take bus 14 or 17 to Sentrum. The bus stop is located just next to the museum.

Website: https://nordlandsmuseet.no/en/citymuseum

Exploring contemporary art
Kaviar factory (Henningsvaer):
This world-renowned art center, located in a former caviar factory, hosts outstanding contemporary art shows. Enjoy the unusual atmosphere and thought-provoking paintings by known and upcoming artists. Located in Henningsværvågen 8, 8300 Henningsvær. An admission charge applies.

Opening/Closing hours: May-September: Daily 11:00 AM - 5:00 PM, October-April: Friday-Sunday 12:00 PM - 4:00 PM.

Getting there: Henningsvær is a tiny community reachable by automobile via the E10 highway and Fv835 road. There is little parking in the town, so park outside and walk inside.

Public transportation: From Leknes Airport, take bus 180 to Henningsvær. The bus station is about a 5-minute walk from the Kaviar Factory.

Website: https://kaviarfactory.com/

Galleri Lofoten (Henningsvær): This gallery, housed in a traditional "rorbuer" cabin, features modern visual art by renowned Norwegian and worldwide artists. Located in Henningsværvågen 52, 8300 Henningsvær. Admission is free.

Opening/Closing hours: May-September: Daily 11:00 AM - 6:00 PM, October-April: Saturday 12:00 PM - 4:00 PM.

Getting there: Follow the guidelines for KaviarFactory above.

Website: [https://m.facebook.com/StudioFellKunst/photos/the-little-carbuncle-comes-along-to-the-role-play-convention-in-cologne-rpc-role/969533596563476

Unveiling Local Gems:
Lille Kabelvåg art gallery and museum (Kabelvåg): Discover local art with historical displays portraying life in Kabelvåg throughout the centuries. Located Storgata 81, 8300 Kabelvåg. Admission charge required.

Opening/closing hours: June-August: Open daily from 11:00 AM until 4:00 PM.

Getting there: Kabelvåg is a bigger hamlet than Henningsvær and may be reached by automobile or public transit. Take the E10 freeway to the Fv833 road. There is parking accessible in the town center.

From Leknes Airport, take bus 180 to Kabelvåg. The bus stop is located immediately next to the gallery and museum.

Website:
https://visitlofoten.com/en/activity/gallery/lille-kabe lvag/

Galleri 2 (Kabelvåg): This artist-run gallery presents rotating exhibits displaying diverse media and techniques, representing the variety of Lofoten's art scene. Located in Kirkegata 2, 8300 Kabelvåg, admission is free. To reach Lille Kabelvåg art gallery and museum, follow the instructions provided above.

Opening/Closing hours: varies based on shows. Stay up-to-date by visiting their website or Facebook page.

Traditional Festivals and Culinary Events

Beyond its beautiful scenery and quaint fishing communities, the Lofoten Islands are alive with a dynamic energy, which is celebrated via distinctive and fascinating traditional festivals. From celebrating the abundance of the sea to remembering Viking ancestry, these celebrations provide an opportunity to feel the genuine character of Lofoten and interact with its rich cultural tapestry. Pack your spirit of adventure and prepare to immerse yourself in the island's bustling calendar.

1. Våganok Traditional Music Festival (Kabelvåg, Late January): This yearly festival allows you to immerse yourself in the fascinating sounds of local folk music and dancing. Observe skillful musicians playing traditional instruments such as the "hardingfele" (violin) and "lur" (trumpet), while dancers in colorful costumes perform lively footwork and storytelling with movement.

Experience live performances at Kabelvåg venues, learn traditional dances in workshops, and soak up the joyful atmosphere with local pride. Don't pass up the opportunity to try wonderful local cuisine and warm yourself with hot drinks among the winter cold.

2. Lofoten Winter Festival (Svolvaer and Kabelvåg, February): Celebrate the magic of winter in Lofoten with this week-long festival full of activities. Witness exciting snowmobile races along icy fjords, go dog sledding, and marvel at lit ice and snow sculptures.

Immerse yourself in a winter paradise with activities like ice skating, traditional games, and cultural celebrations. Enjoy local specialties like "fiskekaker" (fish cakes) and warm yourself with mugs of "gløgg" (mulled wine). Don't miss the beautiful fireworks show that illuminates the night sky above the harbor.

3. Cod Tongue Festival ("Torsketunger Festivalen") (Rien, March): This unique celebration honors an important component of Lofoten's culinary heritage: the cod tongue! Try many versions of this unusual meal, watch the "cod tongue toss" competition, and enjoy live music and entertainment.

Experience the distinct tastes of cod tongue served in conventional and inventive ways. Participate in entertaining events such as speed-eating or the longest peel, and enjoy the vibrant environment of laughing and local spirit. Don't miss out on exploring Reine, a delightful town decorated for the holidays.

4. Lofoten International Art Festival (Kabelvåg, Biennially in June): Experience a contemporary art event that turns Kabelvåg into a thriving art hotspot. Explore creative installations, watch compelling performances, and interact with artists from all around the globe.

Wander around art exhibits held in unusual locations such as disused fish factories and historical structures. Participate in workshops and artist lectures to obtain a better understanding of the creative process. Take in the vibrant environment with other art aficionados while enjoying live music and food sellers.

5. Midnattsol (Midnight Sun), during the summer: Witness the fascinating phenomena of the sun not setting for weeks throughout the summer months. Experience 24-hour sunshine, many outdoor activities, and a distinct vibe that remains in the air.

Enjoy walks and kayaking beneath the midnight sun, attend outdoor festivals and concerts, and marvel at the magnificent play of light on the majestic scenery. Enjoy lengthy nights filled with laughing and bonfires, making memorable memories under the limitless summer sky.

6. Lofoten Matfestival (Food Festival), During the Summer: Enjoy a gourmet trip around Lofoten with this festival exhibiting the finest local vegetables and delectable seafood. Explore food booths packed with delicacies such as "rakfisk" (fermented fish) and "komle" (potato dumplings), and watch famous chefs perform culinary demonstrations.

Try a range of cuisines from various sections of Lofoten, learn about traditional food preparation techniques, and take part in cooking classes to develop your abilities. Enjoy live music and entertainment, creating a joyful environment to celebrate the islands' wealth.

Local Crafts and Souvenirs

Bringing Home a Piece of Lofoten: Discovering Local Crafts and Souvenirs

Lofoten's allure goes beyond its breathtaking scenery and lovely settlements. The islands have a strong tradition of craftsmanship, with unique souvenirs that capture the essence of the place and its people. From hand-knitted woolens to delicately carved wood, your souvenir quest might turn into a treasure trove of genuine findings. Here's how to navigate the local artisan scene:

Knitting Delights:
Wool Sweaters: Cozy sweaters, caps, and mittens are made from Lofoten wool, which is noted for its warmth and durability. Expect pricing to vary from 200 NOK for minor things to 1500 NOK for detailed sweaters, depending on size, intricacy, and yarn quality. Find them in shops around the islands, with Henningsvaer and Stamsund having a large concentration.

Rosemaling: Traditional ornamental painting on wooden goods such as bowls, spoons, and furniture. Prices vary according to size and complexity, ranging from 50 NOK for little decorations to 5000 NOK for huge, elaborate pieces. Visit art galleries and craft shops in Lofoten, particularly in Kabelvåg and Svolvær.

Woven Wonders:
Rya Rugs: Thick, colorful rugs made from wool provide warmth and heritage to your house. Prices vary by size and intricacy, ranging from around 500

NOK for tiny rugs to several thousand NOK for big ones. Explore the stores in Åsgårdstrand and Stamsund.

Hand-knit stockings: Keep your feet warm with genuine Lofoten wool stockings embellished with traditional motifs. Prices normally vary between 100 NOK and 300 NOK each pair, depending on size and detail. Look for them in souvenir shops and fishermen's markets all around the islands.

Carved creations:

Wooden spoons and utensils: These utilitarian keepsakes are hand-carved from local wood and give a bit of rustic character to your kitchen. Prices range from 50 NOK for little spoons to 200 NOK for bigger utensils, depending on the kind of wood and the complexity of the carving. Find them in craft stores and artisan markets, especially in Henningsvær and Kabelvåg.

Troll figures: With hand-carved wooden troll sculptures, you may bring home a piece of Norwegian mythology. Prices vary by size and intricacy, ranging from around 50 NOK for little figurines to 500 NOK for bigger ones. Explore traditional artisan shops and street vendors across the communities.

Treasures from the Sea

Dried Fish: Try the distinctive Lofoten delicacy, dried cod or "tørrfisk." Available whole or in bits, prices begin at around 100 NOK for modest packs. You may find them in grocery stores, seafood markets, and souvenir shops.

Pearls: Lofoten's frigid seas produce stunning pearls, which are often put in one-of-a-kind jewelry items. Prices vary according on pearl size, quality, and setting, ranging from around 200 NOK for modest earrings to several thousand NOK for intricate necklaces. Explore jewelry shops and art galleries in Svolvær and Kabelvåg.

Beyond the Shops:

Lofoten Matfestival (Food Festival): This festival, held throughout the summer, allows visitors to experience local delicacies while also supporting artisan producers. Discover exotic foods such as jams, honey, and cured meats.

Artist markets: During the summer months, pop-up markets in villages and towns showcase local crafts and artwork. Museums and galleries, such as the Lofoten Museum in Kabelvåg, offer locally manufactured gifts inspired by the island's past.

Day Trip

The Lofoten Islands, an archipelago off the northern coast of Norway, are a refuge for outdoor enthusiasts and environment lovers. Lofoten's stunning scenery, attractive fishing communities, and rich cultural history provide a unique experience for first-time visitors. If you're considering a day trip to this magnificent location, here's a recommended schedule to help you see the finest of Lofoten in a short amount of time:

Morning:
Begin your day at Reine, a charming fishing village perched among high mountains and surrounded by crystal-clear seas. Take a walk around the port, seeing the colorful "rorbuer" (traditional fishermen's cottages) and enjoying the tranquil ambiance.

Hike up Reinebringen, a moderate trail that offers amazing views of the settlement, nearby islands, and the huge Norwegian Sea. The route is well-maintained and takes around one hour to complete.

Following your journey, recharge with a great meal at a nearby restaurant. Sample fresh seafood specialties such as cod tongues or fish soup while enjoying the warm friendliness of the people.

Afternoon:

Visit Henningsvaer, another picturesque fishing village famed for its colorful buildings, tiny alleyways, and active art scene. Explore the galleries and stores, and don't pass up the opportunity to trek to the "Kjeholmen" islet for breathtaking views.

Take a boat ride from Henningsvær to explore the nearby islands and skerries. Experience the spectacular coastline up close, observe seabirds and marine life, and enjoy the cool sea wind.

Visit the Lofoten Museum at Kabelvåg to learn about the island's history and culture. Explore displays that highlight traditional fishing tactics, Viking history, and local crafts.

Evening:

Enjoy a typical Norwegian supper at a restaurant in Kabelvåg. Sample delicacies like "lammefrikassé" (lamb stew) or "komle" (potato dumplings), and absorb in the pleasant environment.

During summer, take a walk along the harbor or hike to a viewpoint to witness the midnight sun, casting an ethereal glow on the landscape. Enjoy a relaxing soak in a hot tub overlooking the sea, available at many hotels and resorts.

LOCAL CUISINE

More than simply a magnificent feast for the eyes; Lofoten also provides a gastronomic excursion that will excite your taste senses. Fresh fish collected in the freezing Arctic seas, substantial meals based on years of tradition, and distinct tastes inspired by the harsh but beautiful terrain - Lofoten cuisine is a mesmerizing combination of simplicity and surprise. Grab your fork, and ready to go on a delightful trip.

Traditional Dishes

6 Must-Try Dishes for Your Lofoten Flavor Adventure

Lofoten Islands are known for their magnificent vistas as well as its distinctive and wonderful food, which is profoundly steeped in their fishing tradition. Prepare to tickle your taste senses with these six traditional recipes that encapsulate the soul of Lofoten.

1. Torsketungefestivalen's Star: Cod Tongues.
Imagine these delicate, light pink tongues that like little scallops. Do not be frightened by the name! Traditionally boiled or steamed, they may be eaten chilled with a creamy mayonnaise sauce or fried for

a crunchy texture. Some daring cooks even roast them.

Expect a subtle, somewhat salty taste and delicate texture. Cod tongues are unexpectedly meaty and melt in the mouth.

A distinctive briny flavor that is both subtle and delightful. Imagine it as a gentler, more delicate form of oysters.

Just the freshest cod tongues, simply cooked to highlight their natural taste. Don't miss the Lofoten Cod Tongue Festival in March for an unforgettable experience!

2. Steaming Comfort: Fiskesuppe (Fish Soup).

A thick, creamy orange broth abounding with pieces of white fish, veggies, and sometimes shrimp. Picture a warm embrace in a bowl.

Fish stock is boiled with vegetables, seasoned with local herbs, and thickened with cream for a delightfully smooth consistency.

Immerse yourself in the ocean's warm, soothing embrace. The creamy broth soothes your spirit, while the delicate fish and veggies provide a welcome textural contrast.

A symphony of fish tastes flows over your tongue. Dill, pepper, and other spices provide depth and richness.

The ingredients are fresh local fish, such as cod, haddock, and salmon, combined with root vegetables, onions, and a dash of cream for enticing richness.

3. A rustic delight: Komle (potato dumplings):

Imagine pillowy soft, golden brown dumplings nestling on a platter, commonly served with stews or seafood dishes.

Mashed potatoes are combined with flour and a touch of salt before being cooked or steamed until they float. Simple at its best!

The soft, somewhat chewy texture is quite delightful. Imagine a comfortable cloud of potato bliss.

Mild and somewhat sweet, the ideal base for savory sauces and stews. Some varieties use herbs or spices to increase complexity.

Ingredients include just good old-fashioned potatoes, flour, and perhaps a bit of butter or milk. Simplicity reigns supreme, highlighting the excellence of local foods.

4. A Taste of History: Tørrfisk (Stockfish)

Do not be startled by what you see! The air-dried cod has a dark brown, almost leathery look. However, don't judge a book by its cover!

This is a classic preservation procedure. Cod is air-dried for months, resulting in a distinct texture and concentrated taste. The initial chewiness fades into a pleasantly soft texture, followed by a rush of powerful, concentrated cod taste. Salty, umami-rich, and complex. The extensive drying process amplifies the natural cod flavor, resulting in a distinct and robust taste.

Ingredients are only cod and time! This age-old approach demonstrates the inventiveness of Lofoten residents in keeping food during hard winters.

5. A Sweet Ending: Blåbaerpai (Blueberry Pie)

Picture a rustic, handmade pie with a golden crust filled with lush, juicy blueberries. The scent alone will make your mouth swim!

A simple filling of wild blueberries sweetened with sugar and thickened with cornstarch, wrapped in a buttery, flaky crust. The warm, melt-in-your-mouth crust contrasts well with the sweet-tart filling. Each mouthful delivers a blast of juicy blueberry flavor.

Sweet and somewhat tangy, with a touch of cinnamon for warmth. The natural sweetness of blueberries shows through, resulting in a light and delicious treat.

The ingredients include freshly harvested wild blueberries, sugar, flour, butter, and cinnamon - a delectable showcase of local foods.

6. Warming Comfort: Fårikål (mutton and cabbage stew): A substantial stew filled with delicate mutton pieces, cabbage wedges, and

creamy sauce. Imagine a warm embrace in a pot, ideal for cold nights.

Mutton and cabbage were slowly cooked with peppercorns and whole allspice for hours, yielding a richly delicious and soothing stew. Some varieties include potatoes or carrots for added heartiness.

The soft mutton breaks apart easily, melting in your lips with each mouthful. The cabbage maintains a small crunch, which provides a nice textural contrast. The thick gravy covers everything in wonderful comfort meal joy.

A delicious and comforting sensation. The mutton's mild gaminess complements the sweetness of the cabbage, while the peppercorns and spices offer a hint of warmth and depth.

Ingredients are mutton, cabbage, peppercorns, whole allspice, and sometimes potatoes or carrots. A simple but very tasty meal that exemplifies the heartiness of traditional Lofoten cuisine.

Recommended Restaurants

Here are five amazing restaurants on Lofoten Island that you should surely visit during your stay, along with their details:

Børsen Spiseri

Børsen Spiseri is a famous fine-dining institution built in a historic fish market building with beautiful views of the Svolvær port. They focus on fresh, seasonal foods produced locally, highlighting the finest of Lofoten's produce. Their menu includes modern Nordic cuisine with unique twists, such as langoustines with fennel and elderflower or reindeer meat with caramelized onions and juniper berries. Their vast wine selection and competent personnel enhance the upscale dining experience.

Location: Svolvær, Kabelvåg Veien 158, 8300 Kabelvåg, Norway.

Opening Hours: Monday to Sunday: 12:00 PM to 11:00 PM.

Price Range: Upscale. Expect to pay between 500 and 1000 NOK per person for a full meal.

Phone Number: +47 92 49 57 57

Restaurant Lofotmat

Restaurant Lofotmat is a pleasant and friendly institution that serves tasty and genuine fish meals. They have a casual but classy setting with breathtaking harbor views. Their cuisine combines traditional Norwegian cooking with a contemporary touch, using fresh, local products. Must-try delicacies include pan-fried cod with brown butter and capers, creamy fish soup, and luscious langoustines in garlic butter. They also provide a wide variety of local beers and wines to accompany your meal.

Location: Kabelvåg, Kaikanten, 8300 Kabelvåg, Norway.

Opening Hours: Monday to Saturday: 12:00 PM - 10:00 PM, Sunday: 12:00 PM - 9:00 PM.

Price Range: Mid-range. Expect to pay between 300 and 500 NOK per person for a main meal.

Phone Number: +47 76 95 10 00

Henningsvær Lysstøperi & Cafe

Henningsvær Lysstøperi & Cafe is a unique idea that combines a historical candle workshop with a nice cafe. Located in the lovely town of Henningsvær, it provides a pleasant setting and excellent harbor views. Their menu includes light nibbles, sandwiches, and delectable baked cakes, all ideal for a relaxed lunch or afternoon break. Try their famed fish soup or the "Lofoten Burger" cooked with local lamb. They also provide a selection of locally roasted coffees and teas for a cozy and relaxed atmosphere.

Location: Henningsvær, Sjøgata 25, 8310 Henningsvær, Norway

Opening Hours: Monday to Friday: 11:00 AM - 6:00 PM, Saturday and Sunday: 11:00 AM - 5:00 PM.

Price Range: Casual. Expect to pay between 150 and 300 NOK per person for a main meal.

Phone number: +47 76 04 13 44.

Anita's Seafood

Anitas Seafood is a popular choice for a fast and tasty seafood supper. It is located directly on the shore in Stamsund and provides a relaxed, no-frills ambiance with excellent harbor views. They are recognized for serving fresh, locally caught fish and seafood in basic dishes such as fish and chips, fish burgers, and fish soup. They also provide a range of snacks and drinks, making it an ideal destination for a low-cost and delicious meal.

Location: Stamsund, Kaikanten, 8360 Stamsund, Norway

Opening Hours: Anitas Seafood in Lofoten Islands is open Monday to Saturday from 11:00 AM to 7:00 PM and closed on Sunday.

Price Range: Cost-effective. Expect to pay between 100 and 200 NOK per person for a main course.

Phone Number: +47 95 79 50 84

Bryggerhuset Restaurant

Located in the middle of Svolvær, Bryggerhuset Restaurant offers a vibrant and contemporary atmosphere. They provide a unique mix of a microbrewery and a restaurant, enabling you to taste their freshly made beers while eating wonderful cuisine. Their cuisine incorporates traditional Norwegian meals with a contemporary touch, using fresh, seasonal ingredients. Must-try delicacies include slow-cooked lamb shank with root vegetables, pan-fried fish with velvety mashed potatoes, and their distinctive "Bryggeri Burger" produced with local cattle. They also provide a large range of their own specialty brews to complement your meal.

Location: Svolvær, Torggata 12, 8300 Kabelvåg, Norway.

Opening Hours: Monday - Wednesday: 12:00 PM - 10:00 PM, Thursday - Saturday: 12:00 PM - 11:00 PM, and Sunday: Closed

Price Range: Mid-range. Expect to pay between 300 and 500 NOK per person for a main meal.

Phone Number: +47 76 95 19 00

NIGHTLIFE AND ENTERTAINMENT

The beauty of the Lofoten Islands goes beyond its stunning scenery. As the sun sets below the horizon, a bustling nightlife emerges, with something for everyone. From comfortable pubs with live music to busy bars and even a glimpse of the Northern Lights, here's your guide to discovering the finest of Lofoten after dark:

Bars and Clubs

Whether you're looking for boisterous pubs, cozy cafés, or intense dance, these four establishments provide distinct experiences to spice up your island vacation.

1. Pub Lofoten (Svolvaer): Pub Lofoten is the vibrant hub of Lofoten's nightlife. Expect a vibrant environment, a wide range of local and foreign beers, and tasty pub cuisine. DJs and live music keep the celebration going into the late hours. It is conveniently located in Svolvær and can be readily found on Google Maps. There is no entrance cost. Drinks cost from 100 to 200 NOK, and food is additional. Open 12:00 PM - 01:30 AM weekdays and 12:00 PM - 03:00 AM weekends.

Website and events:
[https://www.facebook.com/p/Lofoten-Pub1-10005
7397181597/?locale=nb_NO] (check Facebook
page for events).

2. Anker Bryggeri (Svolvær): Craft beer
enthusiasts rejoice! This microbrewery has a
comfortable taproom that features their own brews.
On certain evenings, live music and DJ sets provide
a lively atmosphere in which to enjoy local beers
and excellent music. Google Maps makes it easy to
locate Svolvær as well. The entry price varies based
on the event. For more information, visit their
website or Facebook page. Open 12:00 PM - 11:00
PM weekdays; 12:00 PM - 1:00 AM weekends.
Website and events: [https://anker-brygge.no/en]
(see website for event schedule and ticket
alternatives). Phone: +47 91 52 02 82.

3. Børdalsbua (Kabelvåg): Step back in time at
this historic bar, which is built in a typical
fisherman's hut. Experience a cozy atmosphere with
local brews, and occasional live music evenings add
to the allure. Situated near Kabelvåg, a short drive
from Svolvær. Use Google Maps to get directions.
There is no entrance cost. Drink prices vary from
100 to 150 NOK, and food may be offered. Opened
from 12:00 PM - 01:00 AM weekdays and 12:00
PM - 02:00 AM weekends.

Phone number: +47 76 07 55 55

4. Fru Haugans Kafé (Leknes): This quaint café morphs into a busy bar in the evenings, serving drinks, local beers, and sometimes live music performances. Relax and enjoy the amicable environment among visitors and residents. Located in Lofoten's main town, Leknes. Easy to locate with Google Maps. There is no entrance cost. Drinks vary from 100 to 150 NOK. Open from 11:00 AM - 11:00 PM weekdays; 11:00 AM - 01:00 AM weekends.

Website and events:
[https://www.facebook.com/husetkaffebar/]
(visit the Facebook page for events and updates).

Additional Tips:
- It is essential to drink responsibly and follow restrictions.
- For safe night time traveling, consider using a taxi or designated driver.
- Age restrictions apply (18+ for alcohol).
- Tipping is optional, but appreciated.
- Enjoy responsibly and make lasting memories under the Arctic sky!

Live Music Venues

Lofoten's charm is not limited to its vistas; it also has a strong music scene. From peaceful cafés with acoustic sessions to vibrant clubs with enthusiastic bands, the islands provide something for every music fan.

1. Bar Barents (Kabelvåg): Party the Night Away: This pub evolves into a vibrant music venue, with local and international DJs, live bands, and themed evenings. Prepare to dance to anything from indie rhythms to classic rock under the midnight sun or starry sky. Located in the middle of Kabelvåg, readily accessible by foot from the town center. Taxis are easily accessible if necessary. Storgata 102, 8300 Kabelvåg, Norway is the address.

Entry costs vary according to the event. Call Phone: +47 76 07 77 77 for future events and ticket information. Opening hours: Monday to Thursday: 5 p.m. to 1 a.m.; Friday through Saturday: 5 p.m. to 3 a.m.; and Sunday: closed.

2. Hurtigrutens Hus (Svolvaer): Historic Charm and Live Music: Step back in time at this ancient museum, which has been turned into a cultural center. Immerse yourself in the local music scene by attending frequent live performances by local musicians, ranging from traditional folk music to modern jazz. Situated on the Svolvær port, conveniently accessible by foot or a short taxi ride from any location in town. Strandgata 33, 8300 Svolvær, Norway is the address.

The majority of live music performances are included with general museum entry. Check their website for particular event information and possible extra expenses.

Website: https://www.hurtigrutenshus.no/

Opening hours: Museum hours: Tuesday to Sunday, 11 a.m. to 5 p.m. Live music events vary; check the website for scheduling.

Performing Arts Centers

Unveiling the Stage Lights: Performing Arts Delights in the Lofoten Islands.

Aside from its breathtaking natural beauty, the archipelago is home to a surprising number of performing arts facilities, providing unique cultural experiences for visitors. Here's a full guide on making your journey more theatrical:

1. Kabelvåg Kulturhus (Kabelvåg): This cultural hub is the center of Kabelvåg's creative scene. It has a theater space that hosts a variety of acts, including drama, dance, concerts, and film screenings. Located in the middle of Kabelvåg, readily accessible by foot from the town center. Taxis are easily accessible if necessary. The address is Storgata 100, 8300 Kabelvåg, Norway.

Entry costs vary based on performance. Check their website or Facebook page for forthcoming events and ticket information: https://lofotenkulturhus.no/kulturskolens-sommerfe stival-02-juni---04-juni/

Opening hours: Box office hours are Tuesday through Friday from 12 p.m. to 4 p.m. The opening hours for shows vary; check the website.

2. Leknes Kulturhus (Leknes): This cultural center, located in Lofoten's main town, has a broad range of acts such as theatrical plays, concerts, and dance shows. Located in the heart of Leknes and easily accessible by foot from the majority of lodgings. Taxis are available if necessary. Kong Olav Vs Gate 84, 8320 Leknes, Norway is the address.

Entry costs vary based on performance. Check their website or Facebook page for forthcoming events and ticket information: https://www.meierietkultursenter.no/kulturprogram/

Opening hours: Box office hours: Tuesday through Friday, 11 a.m. to 4 p.m. The opening hours for shows vary; check the website.

3. Hurtigrutens Hus (Svolvaer): This historic cargo port has been converted into a cultural center and museum. It sometimes offers theatrical performances, concerts, and other performing arts activities. Situated on the Svolvær port, conveniently accessible by foot or a short taxi ride from any location in town. The address is Strandgata 33, 8300 Svolvær, Norway.

General museum entry may allow access to some events. However, unique fees for performing arts events may apply. Check out their website for more information: [https://www.hurtigrutenshus.no/] .Opening hours: Museum hours: Tuesday through Sunday, 11 a.m. to 5 p.m. The performance schedule varies; check the website.

4. Galleri Lofoten (Kabelvåg): This art gallery sometimes organizes performing arts events, such as spoken word poetry, performance art, and experimental theater. Located in the middle of Kabelvåg, readily accessible by foot from the town center. Taxis are easily accessible if necessary. Location and address is Storgata 108, 8300 Kabelvåg, Norway.

Entry costs vary according to the event. Visit [https://www.instagram.com/gallerilofoten/]

or [https://www.facebook.com/gallerilofoten/]   to learn about future events and purchase tickets.

Opening hours: Tuesday through Saturday, 12 PM to 4 PM. The opening hours for shows vary; check the website.

Exploring these different performing arts venues will give a new depth to your Lofoten experience, allowing you to appreciate the creative and cultural essence of this enchanting archipelago.

PRACTICAL TIPS

Before you begin your travel, consider these practical recommendations to guarantee a smooth and happy experience.

Language Basics

English is extensively spoken in Lofoten's tourist destinations, understanding a few basic Norwegian words might help improve your experience. It demonstrates respect for the local culture, allows you to engage with islanders, and may even result in a hidden treasure tip! Here's a simple tutorial to help you get started:

Greetings and Essentials:
- Hei: Hello (casual) / Hallo: Hello (formal)
- Ha det bra: Goodbye (casual) / Ha det: Goodbye (formal)
- Takk: Thank you
- Vennligst: Please
- Unnskyld: Excuse me
- Ja: Yes
- Nei: No
- Takk, jeg klarer meg: Thank you, I'm alright.
- Hvor er?: Where is...?
- Kan du snakke engelsk?: Do you speak English?

- Jeg forstår ikke: I don't understand.

Useful Phrases:
- Kan jeg få...? May I have...? (e.g., Kan jeg få regningen? - May I have the bill?)
- Hvor mye koster det?: How much does it cost?
- Jeg elsker Lofoten! I love Lofoten!
- Kan du anbefale noe?: Can you recommend something?
- Er det toalett her?: Is there a toilet here?
- Kan du ta et bilde av meg?: Can you take a picture of me?
- Takk for hjelpen! Thank you for your help!

Currency and Banking

Planning a vacation to Lofoten? While the magnificent scenery and quaint towns will captivate your heart, knowing the local currency and banking system will guarantee a stress-free trip. Here's your entire guide to navigating the financial seas of Lofoten.

The currency:
Lofoten, like the rest of Norway, utilizes the Norwegian Krone (NOK). Bills include values of 50, 100, 200, 500, and 1000 NOK, while coins range from 1 to 50 NOK. Tipping is not required,

but is much appreciated, and may be accomplished by rounding up the bill or leaving a modest amount of cash at the table.

Change Your Currency:
There are many alternatives available for changing your foreign cash to NOK.

Before Your Trip: Before you go, exchange your currency at a local bank or travel agency. Rates may be less competitive than in Norway, but they provide convenience.

At the Airport: Oslo Airport Gardermoen features currency exchange counters, but anticipate somewhat higher rates and shorter hours.

In Lofoten: Several banks and exchange offices in major towns, such as Svolvaer and Leknes, provide currency exchange services. Check their websites or phone to get the most up-to-date pricing and hours. Here are some instances.

SpareBank 1 Nord-Norge:
[https://www.sparebank1.no/nb/nord-norge/privat.html] (Several sites in Lofoten)

DNB:
[https://www.dnb.no/en/about-us/offices/international-offices] (Svolvær, Leknes)

Western Union:
[https://www.westernunion.com/no/en/web/send-mo
ney/start] (many places).

ATMs: ATMs are widely accessible across Lofoten
and provide the most cheap currency rates, however
they may levy international transaction fees. Check
with your bank for particular costs.

Current exchange rates:
As of February 3, 2024, below are some estimated
currency rates:

1 USD = 10.02 NOK, 1 EUR = 11.17 NOK, and 1
GBP = 12.36 NOK.

Exchange rates vary, so check for the most recent
rates before your travel.

Bank Hours:
Banks in Lofoten are normally open from Monday
to Friday, 9:00 AM to 4:00 PM, with some shutting
earlier on Wednesday. ATMs are open all day and
night.

Travel Cards and Payment Methods:
Travel cards: Pre-loaded travel cards such as Revolut or Wise provide easy and typically inexpensive conversion rates.

Credit cards: Major credit cards, such as Visa and MasterCard, are generally accepted in Lofoten. However, smaller businesses and eateries may prefer cash.

Debit cards: Ask your bank regarding foreign transaction fees and ATM withdrawal limitations.

Safety and Health

Lofoten Islands are renowned for their spectacular beauty and hospitable attitude, but being prepared for any eventuality provides a really delightful and stress-free vacation. Here's a complete guide on being safe and healthy on your Lofoten adventure:

Health Standard and services

Beyond the fascinating environment, there is a solid healthcare system in place to ensure your well-being throughout your vacation. Let's look at the healthcare standards and services offered in Lofoten, preparing you for a worry-free adventure:

An Overview of the Healthcare System

Norway has a national healthcare system, and Lofoten meets its high requirements. This implies that both residents and tourists have access to high-quality medical treatment, which is typically subsidized. Public healthcare in Lofoten is mostly supported by taxes, assuring affordability and accessibility.

Hospitals and Medical Centers:

Lofoten (emergency and urgent care): This institution in Leknes offers emergency treatment 24 hours a day, seven days a week to both inhabitants and tourists. Address: Storgata 32, 8320 Leknes. Phone number: +47 76 04 66 00.

Nordlandssykehuset Lofoten (Lofoten Hospital): This regional hospital provides a variety of specialty services, including surgery, internal medicine, and radiology. Address is E6, 8300 Kabelvåg. Telephone: +47 76 95 60 00.

General Practitioners (GPs)

Several general practitioners operate in several Lofoten municipalities, providing consultations and basic medical services. Appointments are suggested; contact information may be obtained on the Norwegian Health Economics Administration's (Helseøkonomiforvaltningen) website:

[https://www.helsenorge.no/].(https://www.helsenor ge.no/)

Pharmacies:

Larger towns, such as Svolvaer, Leknes, and Kabelvåg, have pharmacies ("apotek") that provide both prescription and over-the-counter pharmaceuticals.

Emergency numbers:

To contact emergency medical services, dial 113. For police emergencies, dial 112.

Health insurance:

European Health Insurance Card (EHIC): If you are an EU/EEA citizen or have a Swiss EHIC, display it to save money on various medical treatments.

Travel Insurance: Strongly advised to cover unexpected medical expenditures not covered by your main insurance or EHIC.

Additional Tip:

vaccines: While no particular vaccines are required in Lofoten, check your doctor for individualized advice depending on your itinerary and medical history.

medicines: Bring any required medicines, as well as a doctor's prescription if applicable.

Language: Basic Norwegian words might be useful, however the majority of healthcare workers speak English.

Accessibility: Lofoten has adequate accessibility for those with impairments. If you have any unique requirements, please ask ahead of time.

Health Insurance

Before embarking on your adventure, you must first grasp visitor healthcare and navigate the complexity of health insurance. Here's a full analysis to help you prepare for any unforeseen health situations:

Do you need health insurance in Lofoten?

Norway has a universal healthcare system, although it mainly serves its citizens. As a tourist, you may incur charges for medical treatments unless you have:

European Health Insurance Card (EHIC): If you are an EU/EEA citizen or have a Swiss EHIC, you may save money on some medical services such as consultations, doctor visits, and hospital stays. However, it excludes ambulance services, repatriation, and specialist treatment.

Private Travel Insurance: Highly recommended for all tourists, regardless of country. It covers any medical expenditures not covered by your EHIC, such as ambulance services, emergency evacuation, expert consultations, and dental treatment.

Lofoten travel insurance types:

Basic Travel Insurance: Covers necessary medical expenditures, repatriation, and cancellation fees. Choose this option if you intend to conduct little outdoor activity and expect to be in good health.

Adventure Travel Insurance: Offers more comprehensive coverage for sports-related injuries, search and rescue operations, and greater medical evacuation expenses. Choose this if you want to engage in adventurous activities such as hiking, skiing, or kayaking.

Premium Travel Insurance: Provides the most complete coverage, including pre-existing conditions, dental emergencies, and lost or stolen items. Consider this for the most peace of mind, particularly if you have pre-existing medical issues.

Estimate Costs and Coverage:

Costs vary based on your insurance plan, the sort of medical treatment you need, and the provider. This is a preliminary estimate:

- Doctor's consultation: €50-€100 (EHIC may lower costs)
- Hospital stay: Costs vary based on therapy but may reach several thousand euros.
- Emergency evacuation: Thousands of euros, even tens of thousands in difficult cases.

Choosing the Right Insurance:

- Review your current health insurance for abroad coverage and limitations.
- Compare travel insurance companies to find policies that fit your budget, activities, and desired level of coverage.
- Please read the small print. Clarify limits, limitations for pre-existing conditions, and claim procedures.
- Consider extra coverage options, such as dental, cancellation, and lost luggage insurance, based on your requirements.

Suggestions for Using Health Insurance in Lofoten:

- Always carry your EHIC card or travel insurance policy documentation with you.

- Contact your insurance provider right away. If you need medical treatment, contact your insurance carrier as soon as possible to begin the claim process.
- Keep all medical bills, medicines, and receipts for reimbursement.
- Use emergency numbers. In an emergency, phone 112 for rapid medical help.

Security Standard and services

However, before embarking on your travel, you should educate yourself with the security environment and accessible services to guarantee a smooth and worry-free experience.

General safety

Lofoten is usually a safe and pleasant environment, with low crime rates. However, it is always advisable to be alert and take simple precautions:

- Always keep a check on your things in busy areas. Be careful of your surroundings, particularly at night.
- Respect private property and posted signs.Use common sense and trust your instincts.

Emergency Service:

To contact emergency medical services, dial 113. For police emergencies, dial 112.

Fire: Call 110 if you observe a fire or need fire assistance.

Police Stations

While Lofoten does not have typical police stations in every hamlet, there are numerous sites where you may locate police officers or report an incident:

- The address of the Leknes Police Station is Storgata 28, 8320 Leknes. Phone number: +47 76 04 66 00. Monday-Friday, 8:00 AM to 4:00 PM.

- The address for Svolvaer Police Station is Torggata 14, 8300 Kabelvåg. Phone number: +47 76 95 15 50. Monday-Friday, 8:00 AM to 4:00 PM.

- The address for the Stamsund Police Station is Storgata 10, 8360 Stamsund. Phone number: +47 76 04 66 00. Hours are limited; please contact me for further information.

Lost & Found:
If you lose anything in Lofoten, contact the local police station or tourist information center. Tourist information centers can also assist you contact local authorities if necessary.

Additional Tip:
Learn basic Norwegian phrases: Knowing a few important words like "hjelp" (help) and "politi" (police) might be beneficial in emergencies.

Bring a charged phone and a power bank: This guarantees you can contact emergency services if required.

Stay informed about weather predictions to avoid safety risks. Respect local customs and traditions for a pleasant experience for both you and the islanders.

ITINERARIES

Lofoten has something for everyone. Whether you're planning a quick weekend break or a longer trip, here are some itineraries to help you make the most of your visit:

Short Weekend Escape

Lofoten Island Family Escape: A Three-Day Itinerary for Memorable Experiences

---

This itinerary is ideal for a quick weekend getaway with your family, with must-see sights, hidden treasures, and delectable eating experiences. Prepare to make wonderful experiences among breathtaking scenery, quaint towns, and a lively culture.

Day 1: Arrive in Svolvaer and Explore the Town
Morning: Arrive in Svolvær, Lofoten's main town, and check into your accommodations. Enjoy a great breakfast at Svolvær Bakeri, with fresh pastries and local coffee.

Afternoon: Take a walking tour of Svolvær to see its colorful waterfront, lovely shops, and art galleries. Kids will enjoy identifying the funny cod sculptures strewn across town. Don't miss the

Lofoten Islands Museum, which highlights the region's rich history and culture.

Hidden Gem: Take a short detour to Kvalvika beach, which is only accessible by foot or boat. This hidden sanctuary has a beautiful white beach, turquoise seas, and spectacular vistas, ideal for a family picnic and fun.

Evening: For a fantastic seafood feast, visit Bør Dalsbua, a historic tavern located in a typical fisherman's hut. The warm environment and local delights will have you wanting more.

Day 2: Reine, Henningsvær & Viking Adventures

Morning: Rent a vehicle and travel along the beautiful E10 to Reine, a picturesque fishing hamlet noted for its red and white cottages. Hike up the Reinebringen for panoramic views of the Reinefjord, a must-do activity for daring families.

Afternoon: Continue to Henningsvær, a lovely community called the "Venice of Lofoten" for its colorful stilted dwellings. Explore the waterfront, see art galleries, and have lunch at Aalan Restaurant, which is noted for its superb fish and chips.

Hidden Gem: Visit Eggum Beach, which is famed for its fine pebbles and blue seas. Kids will enjoy skipping stones and making sandcastles, while parents may rest and take in the breathtaking surroundings.

Evening: Immerse yourself in Viking history at the Lofotr Viking Museum. Explore rebuilt Viking dwellings, learn about their way of life, and participate in classic Viking pastimes like archery and ax throwing.

Day 3: Kayaking, Nusfjord, and Farewell Dinner.

Morning: Set off on a kayaking excursion through the protected waters of Nusfjord, a lovely fishing community with colorful buildings and traditional fishing boats. Glide along the lovely port, observe marine life, and enjoy the quiet of this hidden treasure.

Afternoon: Explore Nusfjord on foot, stopping at the Nusfjord Fishing Village Museum to learn about the region's fishing legacy. Children will enjoy engaging with friendly farm animals at the Nusfjord Dyregård petting zoo.

Evening: Have a goodbye supper at Anita's Restaurant in Svolvær, with spectacular views of the harbor and great local food. Enjoy fresh fish and traditional Lofoten lamb, and finish your journey on a high note.

One Week Adventure

Prepare for a week of challenging adventure, magnificent scenery, and cultural immersion on the lovely Lofoten Islands! This schedule offers an incredible mix of outdoor activities, cultural encounters, and hidden jewels to ensure your Lofoten journey is memorable.

Day 1: Arriving at Svolvaer
Morning: Arrive at Svolvær, the busy hub of Lofoten. Gear up at a nearby outdoor shop (such as Anton Sport) and have a full breakfast at Vertshuset.

Afternoon: The Svolværgeita climb is an approachable way to experience the majesty of Lofoten. Take in panoramic views of the town and the neighboring islands. Afterward, visit the Lofoten Museum to learn about the local fishing tradition.

Evening: Breivik Brygga offers a spectacular view of the sunset over the harbor. Enjoy real seafood at Restaurant Sjømat & Vinbaren.

Day 2: Reinebringen, and Beyond

Morning: Complete the legendary Reinebringen walk, which rewards you with stunning views of Reine, the Reinefjord, and beyond. Pack a picnic lunch to enjoy the views from the peak.

Afternoon: Visit the picturesque fishing town of Reine. Wander around colorful buildings, stop by Galleria Ny Lofoten for modern art, and hire kayaks for an exciting fjord adventure.

Evening: Relax in the peacefulness of Nusfjord, a preserved fishing community. Stay in a traditional cabin (e.g., Nusfjord Rorbuer) and dine on wonderful Lofoten fish soup at Gammelby.

Day 3: Moskenes and Surfing Adventure

Morning: Head north to Moskenes, which is noted for its stunning scenery and surfing chances. Choose a beginner-friendly surf school (such as Lofoten Surfing) and ride your first wave!

Afternoon: Hike the tough but rewarding Ryten summit near Moskenes, which provides superb views of the coastline and nearby islands. After that, replenish with local beers at Moskenes Bryggeri.

Evening: Take a soothing dip in the natural hot springs of Eggum, surrounded by breathtaking surroundings.

Day 4: Værøy Island and Bird Watching Paradise

Morning: Take a boat to Værøy Island, a popular bird watching destination. Puffins, gannets, and other seabirds may be seen on guided trips such as the Lofoten Sea Safari.

Afternoon: Hike to the Måstad Lighthouse for panoramic views of the island and surrounding waterways. Have a great meal at Værøy Hotel.

Evening: Relax in the island's lone bar, Værøy bar, and enjoy the unique island vibe.

Day 5: Å and Viking History Immersion.

Morning: Drive south to Å, a lovely fishing town with typical red and white homes. Visit the Lofotr Viking Museum, an outdoor exhibit highlighting Viking villages and history.

Afternoon: Hike the Festvågtind path for breathtaking views of Å and the neighboring islands. Afterwards, visit the Å Fisheries Museum to learn more about the region's fishing traditions.

Evening: Enjoy a typical Lofoten supper at Brygge Restaurant, nestled in a historic waterfront building.

Day 6: Henningsvær and Kayak Exploration.

Morning: Visit the lovely town of Henningsvær, also known as the "Venice of Lofoten" for its colorful buildings located on little islands. Visit Galleri Lofoten to see modern art shows.

Afternoon: Rent kayaks to explore the protected bays and islets around Henningsvær. Enjoy a picnic lunch on a remote beach while taking in the peaceful ambiance.

Evening: Enjoy excellent seafood and local beers at Bryggerhuset while enjoying the bustling environment of Henningsvær.

Day 7: Farewell and Svolvær Delights.

Morning: Explore the beautiful waterfront and shops of Svolvær to reflect on your Lofoten experience. Collect one-of-a-kind mementos to commemorate your vacation.

Afternoon: Visit the Hurtigrutens Hus, a historic shipping terminal turned cultural center and museum. Enjoy your final Lofoten meal at Restaurant Sjømat & Vinbaren, which offers spectacular harbor views.

Evening: As you go, take a last sunset boat across Lofoten, soaking in the magnificent surroundings and cherishing the memories you've made.

ADDITIONAL RESOURCES

Planning your Lofoten excursion might be just as fascinating as the trip itself! To ensure you have all the information you need for a seamless and great trip, here are some more resources at your disposal:

Useful Websites

Your Lofoten journey is beckoning, and wouldn't you know it, the internet is full of tools to help you make it unforgettable! To traverse the internet waves and arrange your ideal vacation, here are some crucial websites to bookmark:

Official Tourism Powerhouses:
Visit Lofoten: [https://visitlofoten.com/en/]
The official tourist website is your one-stop shop for everything from lodging listings and activity suggestions to event calendars and transit alternatives. Think of it as your Lofoten trip guidebook!

Lofoten Islands (wikipedia):
[https://en.wikipedia.org/wiki/Lofoten]
A more in-depth look at the islands' history, geography, and cultural significance. Ideal for

fulfilling your wanderlust and discovering the local character.

Conquering the Transportation Jungle

Hurtigruten: [https://www.hurtigruten.com/en-us]
Is a ferry company that connects mainland Norway to the Lofoten Islands, providing spectacular coastline cruises. Imagine the salty wind and stunning scenery when you arrive!

Widerøe: [https://www.wideroe.no/en]
Is a Norwegian airline that offers domestic flights and connects with Bodø, the entrance to Lofoten. Soar over the spectacular scenery and arrive quickly.

Entour Nordland:
[https://visitlofoten.com/en/topic/bus/] Your public transportation guide to buses and ferries in Lofoten and the neighboring regions. Plan your island-hopping trips with ease!

Accommodation Adventures:

Booking.com: [https://www.booking.com/]
A trusted resource for locating hotels, guesthouses, and other lodging options.

Airbnb: [https://www.airbnb.com/] Find unusual and attractive accommodations, such as traditional cabins, that are ideal for immersing yourself in the local culture.

Visit Lofoten. Accommodation: Visit http://www.visitmylofoten.com/stay. A handpicked collection of diverse lodging alternatives, ranging from budget-friendly to luxury, to fit your travel preferences.

Exciting Activities and Tours:

Lofoten Aktiv: [https://www.lofoten-aktiv.no/en/] Your one-stop shop for outdoor experiences, including kayaking, surfing, hiking, and fishing. Get your adrenaline flowing and explore the islands in an active manner!

The Lofoten Adventure:
[https://lofotentours.com/tour/lofoten-in-winter-copy/] Provides guided hikes, fishing expeditions, and other adventure activities for all interests and skill levels. Allow the pros to show you the hidden jewels!

The Lofoten Sea Safari:
[https://visitlofoten.com/en/topic/rib-and-sea-safaris-in-lofoten/] Take a wildlife viewing cruise to see puffins, whales, and other marine species in their natural environment. Prepare to be astonished!

Beyond the Basics:
The Norwegian Meteorological Institute: [https://www.met.no/en/weather-and-climate] Stay on top of the weather with official predictions for Norway, including Lofoten. Pack wisely to prevent any shocks!

Northern Lights Forecast: [https://site.uit.no/spaceweather/data-and-products/aurora/] Have you ever wanted to see the spectacular aurora borealis? Check this webpage for the possibility of witnessing the Northern Lights during your vacation. Keep crossing your fingers!

Books and Films about Lofoten

Books on Lofoten

Lofoten, by Kristin Lofran: This award-winning book provides a thorough reference to Lofoten, covering everything from history and culture to geology and animals. Lofran, a local journalist, offers interesting analysis and practical advice for organizing your vacation.

Islands of Light and Fury by Victoria Moore: This poetic and evocative book looks at the history and culture of Lofoten through the eyes of its inhabitants. Moore, a British journalist who has lived in Lofoten for many years, shares the experiences of fishermen, artists, and other islanders, providing a unique viewpoint on this remarkable location.

The Mermaid of Lofoten, by Erik Fosnes Hansen: This book, set in the nineteenth century, follows the life of a young lady convicted of witchcraft. It's a well written and intriguing story that portrays the raw beauty and distinct culture of Lofoten.

Lofoten, by Jens Christian Leer: This photographic book has breathtaking photographs of Lofoten's scenery, people, and culture. It's an excellent way to gain a feel for the islands before visiting, or to relive your journey after you've returned home.

Midnight Sun by Lars Mytting: This tale takes place in the imaginary Lofoten settlement of Altøygård. It's a dark and frightening narrative about a family split apart by secrets and deception.
[Image of the book Midnight Sun by Lars Mytting.]

Films about Lofoten

Homesick (Hjemlengsel) by Vibeke Janes This documentary chronicles the lives of three persons who have returned to Lofoten after living elsewhere for many years. It's a poignant and enlightening look at the hardships and benefits of living in such a distant and beautiful location.

Jørgen Lorentzen's King Curling: This comedic film takes place in Lofoten during the annual Lofoten Masters curling event. It's a cheerful and humorous look at the islanders' lifestyle and the eccentric personalities that arrive to play in the tournament.

Roar Uthaug's The Wave (Bølgen): This catastrophe film is set in a tiny village in Norway that is devastated by a massive tsunami. It's a fascinating and suspenseful picture that will have you on the edge of your seat. While not recorded on Lofoten, it portrays the majestic majesty of Norway's shoreline.

Lofoten has inspired numerous novels and films, and here are just a handful of them. With its breathtaking beauty, rich history, and distinct culture, it's no surprise that this archipelago has piqued the interest of so many artists and authors. I hope this list helps you decide what to read or watch before or after your vacation to Lofoten.

Maps and Navigation Tools

Here's a thorough reference of maps and navigation tools to assist you easily travel the Lofoten Islands.

Physical Maps:

Lofoten, Turkart: This comprehensive map depicts the whole Lofoten archipelago, including hiking paths, campgrounds, and other spots of interest. It is accessible at the majority of Lofoten's tourist information centers and bookshops.

Norwegian Travel Atlas: This larger-scale map shows all of Norway, including Lofoten. It's important for organizing your vacation and obtaining a feel of the area's topography.

Digital Map and Navigation Apps:

Maps.me: This free software provides offline maps, which you may download before your journey. It contains hiking paths, areas of interest, and information on public transit.

Google Maps: While not always accurate offline, Google Maps is useful for basic navigating in cities and villages. It also provides real-time traffic and public transit information.

Gaia GPS: This software is popular among hikers and outdoor lovers. It provides topographic maps, offline navigation, and the option to trace your path.

UT.no: This software from the Norwegian Trekking Association has extensive hiking maps and route descriptions for all of Norway, including Lofoten. It is accessible in English and is an excellent tool for organizing your hiking trips.

Additional Tip:
- Download maps and navigation applications ahead of time for offline access.
- Bring a portable charger to keep your phone charged while traveling.
- Bring a compass: A compass may help you navigate if you get lost.
- Ask for directions: Locals are nice and helpful, so don't be afraid to ask for instructions.
- Be alert of your surroundings: Pay attention to trail markers and markings, as well as the weather.

Contact Information

Venturing into the gorgeous Lofoten Islands necessitates keeping some handy contact information for unexpected emergencies or just making the most of your vacation. Here's your customized cheat sheet:

Emergency Service:
Emergency Number: 112 (for any emergency, including fire, ambulance, or police)
Police: +47 61 88 00 00 (non-emergency situations)
Medical Services: Leknes Hospital: +47 76 05 60 00 (main number)

Tourism Information:
- Lofoten Tourist Information: +47 76 07 05 75 (Svolvaer)
- Vestvågøy Tourist Information: +47 48 17 50 99 (Leknes)
- Flakstad Tourist Information: +47 91 32 09 03 (Ramberg)
- Moskenes Tourist Information: +47 90 52 07 74 (Reine)
- Værøy Tourist Information: +47 75 42 06 00 (City hall/Ferry pier)
- Røst Tourist Information:+47 76 05 05 00 (City hall/Ferry pier)

Transportation:
- Hurtigruten Ferry: +47 55 55 30 00
- Widerøe Airlines: +47 23 10 75 00
- Entur Nordland (Public Transport): +47 17 79 00 00.

Other Important Numbers:

- Airport Information (Bodø): +47 75 50 73 00
- Currency Exchange: Svolvær SpareBank: +47 76 06 07 00

CONCLUSION

Farewell, Lofoten: A Fond Adieu to a Magical Archipelago.

As the ship leaves the port, throwing Lofoten's craggy peaks into the distance, a bittersweet twinge tugs at my heartstrings. This archipelago, with its spectacular vistas, quaint fishing towns, and welcoming people, has weaved its enchantment into the fabric of my recollections. But as I flip the last page of this guidebook, I'm saying goodbye not just to the island, but also to an experience that has challenged my limits, filled my senses, and left me wanting more.

Sure, the logistics have been taken care of - boat tickets have been purchased, accommodations have been arranged, and must-see locations have been identified. However, Lofoten's genuine gems lie outside the schedule. They may be discovered in unexpected interactions, such as a seasoned fisherman giving tales of amazing catches, a local artist providing insight into their creative process, or shared laughter with other tourists gathered around a blazing campfire beneath the midnight sun.

Remember that trip up Ryten, when the panoramic view took my breath away, the wind whipped through my hair, and the salty taste of the sea energized my soul? Or the peaceful kayak trip across crystalline fjords, punctuated only by the repetitive dip of paddles and the screech of birds overhead? These memories, like brushstrokes on a painting, capture the spirit of Lofoten.

Beyond its outward beauty, Lofoten is genuinely unique because of its people. Their kindness, resilience, and connection to the earth are profoundly felt. Whether it's the shopkeeper carefully explaining the complexities of a traditional Lofoten sweater, the restaurant owner bringing up the freshest fish with a grin, or a fellow hiker providing a helping hand on a difficult track, kindness creates an indelible impact.

Lofoten has also challenged me. The changeable weather compelled me to adapt, the harsh terrain tested my physical capabilities, and the linguistic barrier pushed me beyond my comfort zone. But with each difficulty came a feeling of success, a better appreciation for the beauty around me, and a renewed confidence in my own ingenuity.

I end this handbook with great optimism rather than a feeling of finality. I hope these pages have encouraged you to go on your own Lofoten trip, to make your own memories, and to find the charm that is buried in every corner and cranny of this incredible archipelago.

Remember, Lofoten is more than simply a place; it's an experience. It's a location that will challenge, surprise, and leave you wanting more. So, pack your bags, face the unknown, and let Lofoten weave its enchantment into your tale.

And while you're standing on the ferry deck, waving farewell to this gorgeous island, realize that Lofoten is more than simply a location you visited; it's a part of you, eternally carved in your heart, ready to be rediscovered on your next journey.